THE ULTIMATE MISSOURI TRIVIA QUIZ

MORE THAN 800 QUESTIONS AND ANSWERS ABOUT THE STATE OF MISSOURI

BY ZACH SIMS AND JOHN BROWN

REEDY PRESS
St. Louis, Missouri

Reedy Press
PO Box 5131
St. Louis, MO 63139, USA

Library of Congress Control Number: 2009930946

ISBN: 978-1-933370-82-8

Please visit our website at www.reedypress.com.

cover design by Rob Staggenborg

Printed in the United States of America
09 10 11 12 13   5 4 3 2 1

Photo identifiers:

History
Pony Express
Ferris Wheel, 1904 World's Fair
Nathaniel Lyon

People
Jesse James
George Washington Carver
Josephine Baker

Sports
Buddy Blattner and Dizzy Dean
Casey Stengel
Ed MaCauley

Arts
Tennessee Williams
Langston Hughes
Joseph Pulitzer

Places
University of Missouri Columns
Elephant Rocks
Missouri State Capitol

Business & Politics
Thomas Hart Benton
Anheuser-Busch InBev
Harry S. Truman

Miscellaneous
USS *Missouri*   David R. Francis   Missouri Mule

CONTENTS

INTRODUCTION

MISSOURI IN THE MIDDLE

Missouri has always been a state "caught in the middle." It is located in the middle of the United States, approximately halfway across the country from east to west and north to south. The nation's population center is generally found in the Show Me State, too. Missouri was the twenty-fourth state admitted to the United States of America. The state population of approximately 6 million people ranks twenty-first. When it comes to per capita incomes, Missouri is once again right in the middle, ranking twenty-sixth in the country (in 2006) at $32,705.

We are also generally split in the middle on most political issues. As a matter of fact, we are so entrenched in the middle that Missouri has become known as the "Bellwether State." Oftentimes, the fate of major political issues comes down to how Missourians vote. In the 2008 presidential election, Republican John McCain received 49.39 percent of the vote, while eventual winner, Democrat Barack Obama, scored 49.25 percent. In fact, Missouri has voted in support of the presidential winner in every election but two since 1904.

Missouri itself is, in many ways, a microcosm of the country as a whole. On the east and west boundaries of the state are the major population centers, much like the United States itself. The middle is more rural and less populated. It is more generally socially progressive on the sides and more "down home" in between. We have farmland and plains, mountains and rolling hills, farmland and cities. We grow cotton in the bootheel and make beer in St. Louis. We have Ozark Mountain heritage in the southwest and are a major transportation hub in Kansas

City. Wind farms power entire cities in northern Missouri, and we harness the power of rivers in the middle. Perhaps more than any state, Missouri is a snapshot of America as a whole.

But being in the middle certainly does not mean mediocre. No matter what the category, Missouri proves itself to be a leader. From science to sports, politics to publishing, arts to aviation, the Show Me State has led the way.

One interesting characteristic of Missourians is that they are able to adapt to any situation. As stated, we are diverse in our makeup that very few states can match, which enables us to relate to people in all situations. That trait is evident in two fields in particular: business and broadcasting. It is amazing to look at the sheer number of nationally known broadcasters that hail from Missouri. Television and radio consultants point out that Missourians have no discernable dialect, which is a necessity when broadcasting to the masses across the country. In addition, broadcasters must also be able to relate to people from small towns and big cities, and from all walks of life. That's why many of the legends of broadcasting got their start in the Show Me State. Names like Joe Buck, Walter Cronkite, Rush Limbaugh, Russ Mitchell, Mancow Mueller, Paul Harvey, Stone Phillips, Jann Karl, and Mary Margaret McBride have all made a name for themselves around the country, but they all started in Missouri. In fact, the "father of modern journalism," Walter Williams, grew up in mid-Missouri and wrote the book that is still the basis for the industry today.

Skills that benefit a broadcaster are also the key to success in sales. Business legends like Sam Walton, James Cash Penney, Russell Stover, Edward Jones, Walt Disney, Dale Carnegie, and Adolphus Busch also found success based in their Missouri roots.

In science, we have great minds like James Eads who designed the Eads Bridge. George Washington Carver was raised in rural Missouri and blazed a path through American history that has few rivals.

The political power players that come from Missouri are also an amazing list. Truman, Pendergast, Ashcroft, and Gephardt all dot the political landscape over the past century. Not to mention one of the most influential Socialists in American history, Michael Harrington, also grew up in St. Louis.

In the arts, some of the greatest playwrights, authors, singers and actors all hail from Missouri. George Caleb Bingham, Josephine Baker, Scott Joplin, Charles Russell, and Nelly are all Missourians.

In sports, successful professional teams reside in the state. The Kansas City Chiefs and St. Louis Cardinals dominate their respective leagues. Pro golfers like Hale Irwin, Tom Watson, and Payne Stewart have proven themselves as all-time greats, while being all-time great guys. Then you also have the first family of NASCAR; the Wallaces, along with up-and-comers Jamie MacMurray of Joplin and Carl Edwards of Columbia. Even tennis's Davis Cup was named after a man from the Show Me State, Dwight Davis.

Missouri has towns named Paris, Florida, Nevada, Hayti, Versailles, Vienna, and Houston. We celebrate holidays in small places like Noel. We recognize our freedom in Independence and Republic. We honor our heritage in Chamois and Bois D'Arc.

From Adrian to Zalma and everywhere in between, Missouri has proven itself to be a right in the middle of every major issue and movement over the past three centuries. It is often said that if you want to see a snapshot of how America feels about any particular issue, just look at Missouri. Here we are right in the middle, right where we want to be.

HISTORY

Missouri was admitted into the union as a state with the signing of the "Missouri Compromise" in 1820. That compromise simply meant Missouri was allowed to join the Union as a slave state, while Maine could enter the United States as a free state. But that decision certainly didn't end the debate over slavery in Missouri. As a matter of fact, Missouri's trend to be right in the center of a contentious issue would also be shown once again during the most tumultuous period in U.S. history. The Civil War pitted north against south and brother against brother. In the case of Missouri, North and South went right through our state, both literally and figuratively. Slavery and state's rights divided the state as the Civil War tore Missouri apart at the seams. Decisive battles were fought on Missouri soil, including those at Wilson's Creek, Lexington, Little Blue River, New Madrid, and Boonville.

Some people were proud of Missouri's stand during the Civil War along with war heroes like Ulysses S. Grant, others were enraged at what was happening in the Show Me State. Dozens of well known and notorious outlaws emerged. Names like Jesse James, Bloody Bill Anderson, and William Quantrill became legendary not only in the Midwest, but throughout the United States as well.

World Wars I and II also put Missouri in the spotlight. Hundreds of thousands of soldiers from our state took up the fight for freedom around the globe. Leaders like General John J. Pershing, General Omar Nelson Bradley, and President Harry S Truman all became national heroes and all of them hailed from the Show Me State. Geography once again played a role in Missouri's importance during the World Wars. Because of Missouri's central location, prisoners of war were brought here to be isolated from easy attack on the coasts. Flat topography was also of value for underground missile silos built in western Missouri. A strategic location made the perfect location for United States Air Force training grounds at airfields like Sedalia, Vichy, Malden, and Fort Leonard Wood.

Missouri's strategic central location was such an asset that in the mid-1800s there was a serious effort to move the nation's capitol to the St. Louis area. Washington, D.C., was the logical location for the government headquarters early in United States history. But as the westward migration continued, it became apparent to many that the eastern section of the United States might not be the best place after all. The District of Columbia was located close the ocean, which was viewed as a potential liability for attack. The city had also taken a beating during the War of 1812 with Britain, and much of the infrastructure had been destroyed. Military leaders and politicians began exploring the idea around of moving the government headquarters around 1845, to be near one of the biggest military outposts in the country, Jefferson Barracks.

To many, Jefferson Barracks and the small town of Lemay made a great location for the nation's capitol. It was centrally located along a stretch of the country that was quickly becoming more populous. It was just a few miles away from the city of St. Louis, which had around 5,000 people in 1830 and boomed to more 160,000 by 1860, proving that the area was primed for massive growth. The Mississippi River also ran right next to the town and would make easy access for naval protection and travel. President James Polk also thought it would be good placement since it would be securely protected with such a massive military base so close. However, opposition from both national lawmakers and local leaders derailed the idea, and reconstruction began in Washington, D.C.

HISTORY

THE CIVIL WAR

1. Nathaniel Lyon became the first Union general to fall in the Civil War when he was killed fighting in what southern Missouri battle in 1861?

2. The cannonball lodged in one of the columns of the Lafayette County Courthouse was fired during which Missouri Civil War battle in 1861?

3. What Nevada, Missouri, museum is dedicated to the pro-Southern guerilla bands that operated in Missouri and surrounding states during the Civil War?

4. What southwestern Missouri town was famously sacked and burned by pro-Union Kansas "Jayhawkers" in September 1861?

5. The riot that saw the deaths of twenty-eight people following the Camp Jackson Affair in 1861 in St. Louis came to be known by what name?

6. Approximately how many Civil War battles and skirmishes were fought in Missouri?

    A. 175   B. 550   C. 1,150   D. 1,625

7. What Missouri Civil War battle is known as "the Gettysburg of the West"?

8. After being driven from St. Louis and following a battle with Union troops in Boonville, pro-Southern Missouri Governor Claiborne Fox Jackson set up a temporary government in which southwestern Missouri town in 1862?

ANSWERS

THE CIVIL WAR

1. The Battle of Wilson's Creek

2. The Battle of Lexington

3. The Bushwhacker Museum

4. Osceola

5. The St. Louis Massacre

6. C. 1,150

7. The Battle of Westport

8. Neosho

HISTORY

MILITARY

1. What military installation, located near St. Robert, was built in 1940 and named for a former chief of staff of the United States Army?

2. Which military base, built in 1942 near Knob Knoster, was originally known as the Sedalia Air Force Base?

3. What Air Force base occupied over one thousand acres near Belton from the 1950s to the 1970s?

4. Camp Crowder, which was established in 1941 to serve as the training center for the U.S. Army Signal Corps, was located near which southern Missouri town?

5. Which St. Louis–area military installation served as a major supply station for troops participating in the Mexican-American War?

6. Approximately how many Missourians served in the armed forces during World War II?

> A. 300,000   B. 450,000   C. 600,000   D. 750,000

7. What type of missiles were housed in the approximately 150 underground silos surrounding Whiteman Air Force Base from 1963 to 1995?

8. Navy Admiral Robert E. Coontz, for whom two naval ships have been named, was born in what northeastern Missouri river city in 1864?

ANSWERS

MILITARY

1. Fort Leonard Wood

2. Whiteman Air Force Base

3. Richards-Gebaur Air Force Base

4. Neosho

5. Jefferson Barracks

6. B. 450,000

7. Minuteman missiles

8. Hannibal

HISTORY

THE CIVIL WAR

1. The John Wornall house in Kansas City was used as a field hospital for both Union and Confederate soldiers during which 1861 Civil War battle?

2. The Camp Jackson Affair of 1861 was an armed conflict over the control of what weapons and ammunition cache?

3. In 1863, Union General Thomas Ewing, Jr., issued the infamous "Order No. 11" calling for the depopulation of Bates, Cass, Jackson, and Vernon counties in Missouri in retaliation for what action by Missouri Bushwhackers?

4. One of the earliest armed engagements of the Civil War took place in June of 1861 when a group of Confederate Misssouri State Guardsmen, led by John Marmaduke, was routed by Nathaniel Lyon's Union soldiers at what central Missouri river city?

5. Confederate General Sterling Price, of Missouri, unsuccessfully attempted to establish a colony for ex-Confederate soldiers in what country just after the end of the Civil War?

6. What Confederate calvary leader and Waverly resident led his "Iron Brigade" on a lengthy and disruptive raid into central Missouri in the fall of 1863?

7. A Missouri State Historic Site in extreme northeastern Missouri marks the site of which Union victory of 1861?

8. Confederate General Sterling Price lost almost one thousand men when he raided Fort Davidson during which battle in southeastern Missouri in 1863?

ANSWERS

THE CIVIL WAR

1. The Battle of Westport

2. The St. Louis Arsenal

3. The Lawrence Massacre

4. Boonville

5. Mexico

6. Joseph O. Shelby

7. The Battle of Athens State Historic Site

8. The Battle of Pilot Knob

HISTORY

GENERAL

1. Approximately how many German and Italian prisoners of war were held in Missouri during World War II?

    A. 750   B. 7,200   C. 15,000   D. 22,500

2. Abraham Lincoln, Ulysses S. Grant, Andrew Johnson, Jefferson Davis, Sterling Price, P. T. Barnum, and Charles Dickens were all once guests at what historic St. Louis hotel?

3. Meredith M. Marmaduke and John S. Marmaduke are the only father and son to hold which Missouri political office?

4. What Indian tribe, whose name means "one who has dugout canoes," lived near the confluence of the Grand and Missouri rivers in central Missouri?

5. What explorer, for whom a famous Colorado mountain is named, began his expedition to the American West in St. Louis in 1806?

6. The U.S. Navy battleship U.S.S. *Missouri* is currently retired and on display where?

7. 3,149 square miles of land in northwest Missouri were purchased from the Ioway and the Sac and Fox Indians for $7,500 in what 1836 land deal?

8. What future assassin was arrested in St. Louis in 1862 for making anti-government remarks?

9. Fraternity houses on the University of Missouri campus were used to house a number of foreign POWs taken during which war?

ANSWERS

GENERAL

1. C. 15,000

2. The Planter's House

3. Governor

4. The Missouri (or Missouria) tribe

5. Zebulon Pike

6. Pearl Harbor, Hawaii

7. The Platte Purchase

8. John Wilkes Booth

9. World War II

HISTORY

INFAMOUS

1. The Missouri Bushwhackers who killed more than 150 people and burned much of Lawrence, Kansas, to the ground during the Lawrence Massacre of 1863 were led by what notorious guerilla leader?

2. What Lee's Summit–area native—along with his brothers, Jim, John, and Bob—joined with Frank and Jesse James to form an outlaw gang responsible for multiple robberies and killings across the Midwest in the late 1800s?

3. In 1933, two police officers were killed in Joplin during a shoot-out with members of what notorious Depression-era gang?

4. What 1880s vigilante group took its name from the description of treeless mountaintops located in their part of the Ozarks in south Missouri?

5. William "Bloody Bill" Anderson grew up in what small town in central Missouri's Randolph County?

6. Four peace officers and convict Frank Nash were all killed during what famous shootout in Kansas City on June 17, 1933?

7. Several female family members of Missouri Civil War guerillas were killed in a jail collapse in what Missouri city in 1863?

8. Bushwhacker William "Bloody Bill" Anderson is buried in the Pioneer Cemetery in which Ray County town?

9. Which gang perpetrated the first train robbery in Missouri at Gad's Hill in 1874?

ANSWERS

INFAMOUS

1. William Quantrill

2. Cole Younger

3. The Barrow Gang

4. The Bald Knobbers

5. Huntsville

6. The Union Station Massacre (Sometimes known as the Kansas City Massacre)

7. Kansas City

8. Richmond

9. The James-Younger Gang

HISTORY

GENERAL

1. Winston Churchill's famous "Iron Curtain" speech was delivered on the campus of which Missouri college in 1946?

2. The U.S. government acquired the land that now makes up the state of Missouri as a part of what 1803 land deal?

3. What major event took place aboard the U.S. Navy battleship U.S.S. *Missouri* on September 2, 1945?

4. Which man's landmark legal fight for freedom from slavery in St. Louis was eventually lost in the U.S. Supreme Court in 1857?

5. What 1820 political decision allowed Missouri to enter the union as a "slave" state while at the same time allowing Maine to join as a "free" state?

6. Five Missouri volunteers were among the hundreds of Americans killed during what famous Mexican-American War battle in 1836?

7. In 1870, two steamboats, the *Natchez* and the *Robert E. Lee*, competed in a world-famous race between New Orleans and which Missouri city?

8. *St. Louis Post-Dispatch* reporter Paul Y. Anderson earned a Pulitzer Prize for his investigative reporting on what infamous government scandal that involved oil drilling on public lands in the 1920s?

9. Missouri's first legislature met in 1821 in what eastern Missouri city? (The city served as Missouri's temporary capital from 1821 to 1826.)

ANSWERS

GENERAL

1. Westminster College

2. The Louisiana Purchase

3. The official surrender of Japan, ending World War II

4. Dred Scott

5. The Missouri Compromise

6. The Alamo

7. St. Louis

8. The Teapot Dome Scandal

9. St. Charles

HISTORY

GENERAL

1. What was officially outlawed in Missouri by Governor Thomas C. Fletcher on January 11, 1865?

2. In what year was riverboat gambling legalized in Missouri?

3. What Missouri State Historic Site located in Clark County in northeastern Missouri was once home to an estimated eight thousand Illinois Indians?

4. An American Revolutionary War battle—the Battle of Fort San Carlos—took place in 1780 in which Missouri city?

5. What St. Louis–area military installation was operated by the United States Army from 1826 until 1946?

6. Approximately how many Missourians participated in the Mexican-American War?

    A. 5,000   B. 10,000   C. 15,000   D. 20,000

7. Robert S. Brookings, who helped found the political think tank the Brookings Institute, was a St. Louis resident and a member of the board of trustees of what university?

8. Members of the powerful Pendergast political faction in Kansas City were known by what animal nickname?

9. Which famous Spanish conquistador is believed to have been the first European to set foot in land that is now Missouri in 1541?

10. The Gratiot Street Prison in St. Louis housed prisoners of war during which conflict?

Answers

General

1. Slavery

2. 1992

3. Illiniweck State Historic Site

4. St. Louis

5. Jefferson Barracks

6. B. 10,000

7. Washington University

8. The Goats

9. Hernando de Soto

10. The Civil War

HISTORY

GENERAL

1. What was the nickname of the large Mississippi River sandbar near St. Louis that was the scene of numerous nineteenth century duels?

2. In 1838, Governor Lilburn W. Boggs issued an "Extermination Order," which called for the removal of members of what religious group from the state of Missouri?

3. What famous explorer acted as the governor of the Missouri Territory from 1813 to 1820?

4. What St. Louis university was first known as Eliot Seminary?

5. What Missourian was the U.S. Military's last five star general?

6. What famous Missouri politician shot future U.S. President Andrew Jackson in the arm during a brawl in Nashville, Tennessee, in 1812?

7. Who was the self-taught engineer and architect who designed and built the combination road and railway bridge across the Mississippi in St. Louis in 1874?

8. Three people were killed and more than four hundred houses and thirty riverboats were lost in a massive fire in what Missouri city in 1849?

9. What legendary blackpowder rifle, extremely popular with trappers and frontiersmen, was manufactured by two St. Louis brothers during the early nineteenth century?

10. The bloodless "Honey War" of 1839 was a boundary dispute between Missouri and what neighboring state?

ANSWERS

GENERAL

1. Bloody Island (The dueling parties used the island because it was technically under the jurisdiction of neither Missouri nor Illinois.)

2. The Latter Day Saints (Mormons)

3. William Clark

4. Washington University

5. Omar Bradley

6. Thomas Hart Benton

7. James Eads

8. St. Louis

9. The Hawken Rifle (Jacob and Samuel Hawken)

10. Iowa

HISTORY

THE CIVIL WAR

1. The Missouri State Guard, led by Claiborne Fox Jackson, defeated the Union forces of Colonel Franz Sigel in what battle fought in southwest Missouri on July 5, 1861?

2. Ten Confederate prisoners of war were executed in which northeastern Missouri town's "massacre" in retribution for the abduction of a Union sympathizer in 1862?

3. Loose Park in Kansas City was the site of much of the fighting of which Missouri Civil War battle?

4. Confederate forces under General Sterling Price successfully raided an arms reserve in which Howard County river town in 1864?

5. Which county reported a total of 6,374 slaves held, the most of any Missouri county, in the 1860 U.S. Census?

    A. Howard County   B. Lafayette County
    C. Pike County   D. Boone County

6. What nickname did Missouri State Guard General M. Jeff Thompson earn for the crafty tactics he used while fighting in the backwaters of southeastern Missouri during the Civil War?

7. Confederate General Sterling Price held what governmental position in Missouri from 1853 to 1857?

8. Which St. Louis–area college's main campus is located at the former site of Camp Jackson?

ANSWERS

THE CIVIL WAR

1. The Battle of Carthage

2. Palmyra

3. The Battle of Westport

4. Glasgow

5. B. Lafayette County

6. "Swamp Fox"

7. Governor

8. Saint Louis University

HISTORY

INFAMOUS

1. What infamous Bushwhacker led the group of guerillas (including Frank and Jesse James) who perpetrated the Centralia Massacre in September 1864? (They executed twenty-two Union soldiers on furlough in Centralia before ambushing and killing one hundred more just outside of town.)

2. What notorious Irish-American gang was founded in St. Louis in the late 1800s by Thomas "Snake" Kinney and Tom Egan?

3. Governor Thomas T. Crittendon put a ten-thousand-dollar bounty on the head of which Missouri outlaw in 1882?

4. Which famous Depression-era gangster is believed to have been one of the gunmen in the Union Station Massacre in Kansas City in 1933?

5. Frank and Tubal Taylor were hanged by what Ozarks vigilante group for the killing of a Taney County shopkeeper and his wife in 1885?

6. What Illinois native, convicted in the assassination of Martin Luther King, Jr., in Memphis in 1968, had escaped from the Missouri State Penitentiary roughly one year before the murder?

7. Which Richmond native shot and killed Jesse James in his St. Joseph home in 1882?

8. What famously ill-fated group of settlers left Independence for California via the California Trail in 1846?

9. Six police officers were killed in what shootout with a group of outlaw brothers near Brookline in 1932?

ANSWERS

INFAMOUS

1. William "Bloody Bill" Anderson

2. Egan's Rats

3. Jesse James

4. Charles "Pretty Boy" Floyd

5. The Bald Knobbers

6. James Earl Ray

7. Robert Ford

8. The Donner Party

9. The Young Brothers Massacre

HISTORY

GENERAL

1. Two sons of Daniel Boone produced and sold salt from a saltwater spring "lick" at the location of which aptly named historic site near Arrow Rock?

2. Two Missouri governors, Meredith M. Marmaduke and Claiborne Fox Jackson, are buried at what historic site near Arrow Rock?

3. What Laclede-born Army general led U.S. forces in World War I as the commander of the American Expeditionary Force?

4. An estimated four thousand Cherokee Indians lost their lives during what forced relocation, which passed through Missouri in the 1830s?

5. U.S. Army Captain Albert Berry is credited with the first parachute jump from a moving airplane in 1912. At what Missouri military installation did he land?

6. What Navy battleship was affectionately known by its crew as the "Mighty Mo"?

7. Which Old West gunfighter from Memphis, Missouri, was portrayed by one-time Slater resident Steve McQueen in a 1980 movie bearing his name?

8. Old West legend Belle Starr was born in February of 1848 in what southwestern Missouri town?

9. The U.S. military's M2 and M3 fighting vehicles are named for what Clark-born U.S. Army general?

ANSWERS

GENERAL

1. Boone's Lick State Historic Site

2. Sappington Cemetery State Historic Site

3. General John J. Pershing

4. The Trail of Tears

5. Jefferson Barracks

6. U.S.S. *Missouri*

7. Tom Horn

8. Carthage

9. General Omar Bradley (The M2 Bradley IFV and the M3 Bradley CFV)

HISTORY

DISASTERS

1. More than one hundred people, including a large number of Mormon immigrants, were killed when what steamboat exploded on the Missouri River near Lexington in 1852?

2. More than 130 St. Louisans died in 1896 as a result of what natural force?

3. Over thirty people, including the grandfather of poet Sara Teasdale, were killed on November 1, 1855, near St. Louis due to the collapse of what structure?

4. One of the most powerful earthquakes ever felt in the United States occurred near what southeastern Missouri town in 1812?

5. Which St. Louis–area community was bought out and permanently evacuated in 1983 because of dioxin contamination?

6. The costliest flood in American history, which devastated large areas of Missouri and surrounding states, occurred in what year?

7. The Tri-State Tornado of 1925, which is the deadliest recorded tornado in American history, touched down near which southeastern Missouri town? (It shares its name with the home of the U.S. Naval Academy.)

8. The first commercial airline bombing in the United States took place aboard a Continental Airlines flight from Chicago to Kansas City in 1962 when a bomb was detonated inside the plane over what northeastern Missouri town?

ANSWERS

DISASTERS

1. *The Saluda*

2. A tornado

3. The Gasconade River Bridge

4. New Madrid

5. Times Beach

6. 1993

7. Annapolis

8. Unionville

HISTORY

GENERAL

1. What famous gunfighter and one-time constable of Lamar, Missouri, was involved in the shootout at the O.K. Corral in Arizona in 1869?

2. The still-visible Indian mounds near the town of East Prairie in southeastern Missouri were built by members of what large Indian group?

3. The Reverend John Berry Meachum of St. Louis started a school in what location in 1847? (The school was located there to skirt a Missouri state law prohibiting the education of African Americans in the state.)

4. A Missouri State Historic Site near Nevada marks the location of a three-thousand-member village of what Indian tribe who occupied the area in the eighteenth century?

5. What legendary Wild West figure and friend of Wild Bill Hickock was born Martha Jane Canary in Princeton in 1852?

6. The Truman family stayed in what historic Washington, D.C., residence while the White House underwent renovations from 1948 to 1952?

7. The Pony Express connected St. Joseph and which California city?

8. What one-time Arrow Rock resident was a politician and artist who gained acclaim for his paintings depicting frontier life in Missouri in the 1800s?

9. What facility, complete with four buildings and a wooden fence, first opened in Jefferson City in 1836?

ANSWERS

GENERAL

1. Wyatt Earp

2. Mississippian

3. A steamboat on the Mississippi River

4. Osage

5. Calamity Jane

6. The Blair House

7. Sacramento

8. George Caleb Bingham

9. The Missouri State Penitentiary

HISTORY

GENERAL

1. In 1939, Owen Whitfield and over fifteen hundred protestors camped along Highway 61 in southern Missouri to draw attention to the living and working conditions of what agricultural trade?

2. Missourian William Becknell established what famous trade route between the United States and what was then Mexico in 1821?

3. The only woolen mill from the 1860s that is still standing is located in what western Missouri State Historic Site?

4. The Russell, Majors, and Waddell partnership operated what Missouri-based mail delivery business?

5. What fort, established in 1723 by Frenchman Etienne de Bourgmont near present-day Brunswick, was the first fort on the Missouri River?

6. Which Florissant-based Jesuit worked as a missionary among the Native American peoples in the early nineteenth century? (A St. Louis–area private school bears his name).

7. A shootout on the town square in Springfield in 1865 helped launch the legend of which famous Old West lawman and gunfighter?

8. What historic site in Hermann illustrates the day-to-day lives of German immigrants in the nineteenth century?

9. The Lewis and Clark expedition left St. Louis on May 14 of what year?

ANSWERS

GENERAL

1. Tenant farming/sharecropping

2. The Santa Fe Trail

3. Watkins Mill

4. The Pony Express

5. Fort Orleans

6. Father Pierre-Jean De Smet

7. Wild Bill Hickock

8. Deutschheim State Historic Site

9. 1804

HISTORY

1904 WORLD'S FAIR

1. The 1904 World's Fair in St. Louis was held to celebrate the centennial of what historic event?

2. Approximately how many people attended the 1904 World's Fair?

   A. 4 million   B. 10 million   C. 20 million   D. 28 million

3. What popular ragtime musician and Missouri resident performed on the Pike at the Fair?

4. A popular exhibit during the Fair was a dramatization of the destruction of what Texas city during a 1900 hurricane?

5. What famous march composer and his band entertained visitors with performances during the Fair?

6. What was the official name of the 1904 World's Fair?

7. Approximately how many buildings were constructed for the Fair?

   A. 550   B. 900   C. 1,200   D. 1,500

8. Who was the president of the Louisiana Purchase Exposition Company?

9. What material was used as the basis of construction for the major Fair palaces?

ANSWERS

1904 WORLD'S FAIR

1. The Louisiana Purchase

2. C. 20 million

3. Scott Joplin

4. Galveston

5. John Philip Sousa

6. The Louisiana Purchase Exposition

7. D. 1,500

8. David R. Francis

9. staff

HISTORY

GENERAL

1. What fort, located near Sibley in western Missouri, was established in 1808 as a government-controlled trading post?

2. Frontiersman and scout Kit Carson grew up in what small Missouri river town located near Boonville?

3. How many Missourians served in the military during World War I?

    A. 100,000   B. 125,000   C. 150,000   D. 175,000

4. How many Missouri casualties were suffered during World War I?

    A. 11,172   B. 16,554   C. 19,332   D. 24,595

5. Pierre Laclede and Auguste Chouteau founded St. Louis in 1764 as a base of operations for what type of business?

6. According to the census taken that year, how many slaves were living in Missouri in 1860?

    A. 46,780   B. 85,500   C. 102,221   D. 114,930

7. What Iowa-born U.S. president owned a farm near Maryville?

ANSWERS

GENERAL

1. Fort Osage

2. Franklin

3. C. 150,000

4. A. 11,172

5. Fur trading

6. D. 114,930

7. Herbert Hoover

Sports

Missouri has an amazing legacy when it comes to professional sports teams and athletes. The Kansas City Chiefs are one of the most storied franchises in professional sports history. The St. Louis Rams and their "Greatest Show on Turf" captivated NFL fans for a number of years. But it's baseball that usually has the state cheering, and divided!

One of the greatest World Series' of all time was practically a battle of Missouri. No, it's not the I-70 Series that was played in 1985 between the St. Louis Cardinals and Kansas City Royals. The series that had perhaps the biggest contribution from Missourians was in 1964: St. Louis versus the dreaded New York Yankees.

On the surface, it was just a battle between two of the winningest professional baseball teams of all time. But a closer look at the rosters shows it was practically a Show Me State homecoming for both teams. In fact, this series could almost have been played out as a Missouri Little League game a few years earlier!

The Cardinals had a roster full of home-grown products. Mike Shannon grew up in St. Louis and was the hometown star. Third baseman Ken Boyer was born in Liberty, Missouri, and grew up in the Kansas City area. Shortstop Dal Maxvill was from Granite City, Illinois, and attended Washington University. Infielder Jerry Buchek and outfielder Charlie James both were born and raised in St. Louis. The manager, Jerry Keane, was also from St. Louis.

The Yankees also had many Missouri products. All-star

catcher Elston Howard grew up in St. Louis and attended Vashon High School. Third baseman Clete Boyer, brother of Ken, was born in Cassville, Missouri, and also grew up near Kansas City. Pitcher Mel Stottlemeyer was raised in Hazelton, Missouri. Even the great Mickey Mantle entertained minor league fans in Joplin early in his career. First base coach Phil Gleason grew up in Kansas City and attended Rockhurst University. The manager of that great Yankees team was none other than St. Louis–born and raised Yogi Berra.

Even the national broadcasters had a Missouri bent. On TV, it was Haray Caray and Curt Gowdy. Caray grew up in St. Louis and was a huge fan of his hometown team. In fact, his boyhood home was just a few blocks from where the present-day Busch Stadium stands. He was the voice of the Cardinals for many years alongside his equally famous partner, Jack Buck.

On the radio calling the game, it was Phil Rizzuto and Joe Garagiola. Garagiola, much like Caray, lived in St. Louis as a child and grew up wanting to be a Cardinal. In fact, he was childhood best friends of Yankees' manager Berra. So for these two long-time friends and competitors, this series was yet another trip to a place they spent many of their childhood days, Cardinals baseball games in St. Louis.

Even Umpire Ken Burkhart played for the Cardinals in the mid-1940s.

In the end, the Cardinals prevailed in seven games, bringing the Redbirds their seventh World Series Championship and ending the Yankees dominance of Major League Baseball for more than a decade. At the conclusion of the series, Berra was fired by the Yankees, who then hired Keane, who resigned from the Cardinals right after the series was over. An amazing turn of events all centered around a group of young men from Missouri.

SPORTS

BASEBALL

1. What Hamilton-born Baseball Hall of Famer starred as an outfielder for the Brooklyn Dodgers from 1909 to 1926? (His Dodger-franchise records for hits, total bases, doubles, and triples still stand today.)

2. What St. Louis beer company was a major sponsor of the St. Louis Cardinals radio broadcast in the 1940s and 1950s?

3. What power-hitting third baseman played college baseball at Northwest Missouri State University before winning a World Series title with the Minnesota Twins in 1987?

4. Which Cardinal great finished his career with 3,630 hits, 1,815 on the road and 1,815 at home?

5. What Springfield native set a major league record by hitting home runs in eight straight games while playing for the Pittsburgh Pirates in 1956?

6. Only the New York Yankees have won more World Series Championships than the St. Louis Cardinals. How many World Series have the Cardinals won?

    A. 6   B. 8   C. 10   D. 12

7. Who was the MVP of the 1985 "I-70" World Series between the Kansas City Royals and the St. Louis Cardinals?

8. What Kansas City native and alumnus of Central High won seven World Series championships while managing the New York Yankees from 1949 to 1960?

ANSWERS

BASEBALL

1. Zack Wheat

2. Griesedieck Brothers Beer

3. Gary Gaetti

4. Stan Musial

5. Dale Long

6. C. 10

7. Bret Saberhagen

8. Casey Stengel

SPORTS

BASKETBALL

1. What legendary Oklahoma State University men's basketball coach was born in Easton, Missouri, in 1904?

2. What Missouri State (SMSU) women's basketball star became the NCAA's all-time leading scorer when she scorred her 3,123rd point in March of 2001?

3. What was the name of the NBA franchise that played in St. Louis from 1955 to 1968?

4. How many Big 8 titles did Missouri Tigers men's basketball teams win?

      A. 5   B. 6   C. 7   D. 8

5. Basketball Hall of Famer Harry Gallatin played college hoops at what northern Missouri school before going on to play in the NBA from 1948 to 1958?

6. In 1955, the basketball facility at the University of Kansas was named for what legendary Jamesport, Missouri-born basketball coach?

7. What former St. Louis area high school basketball star and Kansas Jayhawk was intensely booed every time he touched the ball during games at the Hearnes Center at the University of Missouri from 1996 to 1999?

8. What Crystal City native was a three-time All-American basketball player at Princeton University before playing for the New York Knicks?

ANSWERS

BASKETBALL

1. Henry Iba

2. Jackie Stiles

3. St. Louis Hawks

4. D. 8

5. Truman State University (Then known as Northeast Missouri State Teacher's College)

6. Phog Allen

7. Ryan Robertson

8. Bill Bradley

Sports

Name That Mascot

Match the Missouri university or college with their athletic mascot.

1. William Woods University

2. Truman State University

3. William Jewell College

4. University of Missouri

5. College of the Ozarks

6. Culver-Stockton College

7. Missouri Western University

8. Park University

9. Northwest Missouri State

10. Evangel University

11. Maryville University

A. Cardinals

B. Bobcats

C. Bearcats

D. Owls

E. Wildcats

F. Pirates

G. Crusaders

H. Tigers

I. Griffons

J. Saints

K. Bulldogs

ANSWERS

NAME THAT MASCOT

1. D. William Woods Owls

2. K. Truman State Bulldogs

3. A. William Jewell Cardinals

4. H. Missouri Tigers

5. B. College of the Ozarks Bobcats

6. E. Culver-Stockton Wildcats

7. I. Missouri Western Griffons

8. F. Park Pirates

9. C. Northwest Missouri State Bearcats

10. G. Evangel Crusaders

11. J. Maryville Saints

SPORTS

FOOTBALL

1. What King City native and former MU Tiger All-American defensive back was inducted into the Pro Football Hall of Fame in 2007 after a stellar fourteen-year career with the St. Louis Cardinals?

2. What former AFL team from Texas moved north to become the Kansas City Chiefs in 1963?

3. What standout University of Missouri wide receiver was named an All-American in 1975?

4. In what year did the Rams move from Los Angeles to St. Louis?

5. In what year did the Kansas City Chiefs win their only Super Bowl?

6. What Kansas City native and former University of Missouri football player's last-second tackle of Tennesee Titans receiver Kevin Dyson helped preserve the St. Louis Rams victory in Super Bowl XXXIV?

7. The football team from which central Missouri high school has won a record ten state championships?

8. A number of high school football teams in north and central Missouri compete in what pared-down version of the sport?

ANSWERS

FOOTBALL

1. Roger Wehrli

2. The Dallas Texans

3. Henry Marshall

4. 1995

5. 1970 (Super Bowl IV)

6. Mike Jones

7. Jefferson City High School

8. Eight-man football

SPORTS

NAME THAT MASCOT

Match the Missouri university or college with their athletic mascot.

1. Webster University   A. Panthers

2. Drury University   B. Hawks

3. Missouri State University   C. Tritons

4. Lincoln University   D. Gorloks

5. Central Methodist University   E. Bearcats

6. Southwest Baptist University   F. Blue Tigers

7. UM–St. Louis   G. Kangaroos

8. Fontbonne University   H. Lions

9. Rockhurst University   I. Bears

10. Lindenwood University   J. Griffins

11. UM–Kansas City   K. Eagles

ANSWERS

NAME THAT MASCOT

1. D. Webster Gorloks

2. A. Drury Panthers

3. I. Missouri State Bears

4. F. Lincoln Blue Tigers

5. K. Central Methodist Eagles

6. E. Southwest Baptist Bearcats

7. C. UMSL Tritons

8. J. Fontbone Griffins

9. B. Rockhurst Hawks

10. H. Lindenwood Lions

11. G. UMKC Kangaroos

SPORTS

FOOTBALL

1. What St. Louis native won the Heisman Trophy as a running back for the Oklahoma Sooners in 1978?

2. NFL and University of Missouri football players Justin Gage, Justin Smith, and Steve Martin all played football at what powerhouse high school program?

3. Before moving to River Falls, Wisconsin, the Kansas City Chiefs held their annual training camp on the campus of what Missouri college?

4. What legendary Missouri high school football coach has the fourth most wins of any high school coach in history? (He compiled an incredible 405–60–4 record in forty-four years of coaching at Centralia and Jefferson City high schools.)

5. What consensus All-American from Kirkwood set the NCAA freshman record for all-purpose yards in a season during the 2007 University of Missouri football campaign?

6. What prize goes to the winner of the annual University of Missouri vs. University of Nebraska football game?

7. Long-time Denver Broncos wide receiver Rod Smith played college football at what small Missouri university?

8. What is the name of the college athletic conference that the University of Missouri first joined in 1907? (The original seven teams were Missouri, Nebraska, Kansas, Iowa, Ames, Drake, and Washington University.)

ANSWERS

FOOTBALL

1. Billy Sims

2. Jefferson City High School

3. William Jewell College

4. Pete Adkins

5. Jeremy Maclin

6. The Missouri-Nebraska Bell

7. Missouri Southern State University

8. Missouri Valley Conference

Sports

Football

1. What Texas native was named a football All-American at defensive back for Missouri in 1965, and is one of only seven Tigers to have his jersey (#23) retired?

2. What prize goes to the winner of the annual University of Missouri vs. University of Kansas football game?

3. In which year was the first University of Missouri football team organized?

     A. 1890   B. 1895   C. 1900   D. 1903

4. The Telephone Trophy is given to the winner of the annual football game between the University of Missouri and what other Big 12 North school?

5. What Maplewood-born Missouri Tiger quarterback and two-time All-American led Mizzou to wins in 20 of the 28 games he played in from 1938 to 1940?

6. After the 38–7 season-ending demolition of Arkansas in the 2007 Cotton Bowl, the Missouri Tigers achieved their highest ever final ranking when they were slotted where in the AP poll?

7. Who served as athletic director for the University of Missouri when Norm Stewart was hired to run the men's basketball program in 1967?

8. Who was the first Kansas City Chiefs running back to lead the league in rushing yardage?

ANSWERS

FOOTBALL

1. Johnny Roland

2. The Indian War Drum

3. 1890

4. Iowa State University

5. "Pitchin" Paul Christman

6. 4

7. Dan Devine

8. Christian Okoye, 1989

Sports

Baseball

1. What catcher for the Cardinals, Dodgers, and Cubs returned to his native Missouri in 1959 to open a baseball academy near Miller?

2. What Independence-born pitcher, known as "The Red Baron," won the 1984 Cy Young Award while pitching for the Chicago Cubs in 1984?

3. Reliever Darold Knowles, who holds the unbreakable record of pitching in all seven games of a World Series, was born in which central Missouri town?

4. Which Hall of Fame pitcher from Carthage won 253 games during his sixteen-year career with the New York Giants? (He is well-known for striking out five future Hall of Famers in a row during the 1934 All Star Game.)

5. Two of the four ballplayers in the history of Major League baseball to have collected over 3,000 hits, 300 home runs, and maintained a .300 career batting average played their entire careers for Missouri teams. Who are those two players? (The other two are Hank Aaron and Willie Mays.)

6. What St. Louis Browns owner and promoter sent 3'7" Eddie Gaedel to the plate in 1951?

7. What year were the Kansas City Monarchs disbanded?

8. Born in St. Louis in 1914, what legendary baseball broadcaster called Cardinals games before moving on to become the long-time voice of the Chicago Cubs?

ANSWERS

BASEBALL

1. Mickey Owen

2. Rick Sutcliffe

3. Brunswick

4. Carl Hubbell

5. George Brett and Stan Musial

6. Bill Veeck

7. 1965

8. Harry Caray

Sports

Name That Mascot

Match the Missouri university or college with their athletic mascot.

1. University of Central Missouri   A. Redhawks

2. Harris Stowe University   B. Lions

3. Missouri Southern State   C. Billikens

4. Avila University   D. Cougars

5. Washington University   E. Mules

6. Southeast Missouri State   F. Miners

7. Missouri S&T (UM–Rolla)   G. Bears

8. Saint Louis University   H. Eagles

9. Missouri Valley College   I. Hornets

10. Hannibal-LaGrange   J. Trojans

11. Columbia College   K. Vikings

ANSWERS

NAME THAT MASCOT

1. E. Central Missouri Mules

2. I. Harris-Stowe Hornets

3. B. Missouri Southern Lions

4. H. Avila Eagles

5. G. Washington Bears

6. A. Southeast Missouri Redhawks

7. F. Missouri S&T Miners

8. C. Saint Louis University Billikens

9. K. Missouri Valley Vikings.

10. J. Hannibal LaGrange Trojans

11. D. Columbia College Cougars

SPORTS

MISCELLANEOUS

1. What year did the University of Missouri athletic teams introduce Truman the Tiger as their mascot?

2. What Springfield-born golfer won three majors, including U.S. Open titles in 1991 and 1999?

3. The inaugural running of what professional bicycle race was held in Missouri in September 2007?

4. Members of which St. Louis–area racing family include Mike, Kenny, Steve, and Rusty?

5. Boxer Ken Norton, one of the few fighters to defeat Muhammad Ali, attended what small Missouri college on a football scholarship?

6. Which Kansas City–born golfing legend won eight majors, including five British Open titles, during his long PGA career?

7. The football field at the University of Central Missouri (CMSU) bears the name of what Kansas City–born athlete who starred on the football, track, and baseball teams at Central before moving on to pitch in the major leagues for twelve seasons?

8. NASCAR racing star Carl Edwards was born and raised in which Missouri city?

ANSWERS

MISCELLANEOUS

1. 1984

2. Payne Stewart

3. The Tour of Missouri

4. The Wallace Family

5. Truman State University (Northeast Missouri State University)

6. Tom Watson

7. Vernon Kennedy

8. Columbia

SPORTS

MISCELLANEOUS

1. What popular Quitman-born professional wrestler of the 1970s and 1980s opened a wrestling academy in Eldon following his retirement from pro wrestling?

2. What was the name of the NHL franchise that played in Kansas City from 1974 to 1976?

3. What legendary Mizzou football coach is credited with inventing the "Split T" formation?

4. What sporting event was originally scheduled to take place in Chicago in 1904 but was instead held in St. Louis after threats from World's Fair organizers of setting up a competing event?

5. Three-time U.S. World Cup soccer team member and English Premier League veteran Brian McBride played college soccer at which Missouri university?

6. Callaway County native Helen Stephens, who was a world-famous track athlete and 1936 Olympic gold medalist, was known by what nickname?

7. Basketball players Kareem and Jaron Rush, golfer Tom Watson and two sons of football coaching legend Knute Rockne all attended what private school in Kansas City?

8. Cal Hubbard, the only person inducted into both the pro football and pro baseball halls of fame, hails from what central Missouri town?

ANSWERS

MISCELLANEOUS

1. Harley Race

2. The Kansas City Scouts

3. Don Faurot

4. The Summer Olympics

5. Saint Louis University

6. The Fulton Flash

7. Pembroke Hill

8. Keytesville

SPORTS

MISCELLANEOUS

1. In an era when there were only eight weight divisions in boxing, what St. Louis native held titles to three of them simultaneously?

2. What Shelbyville native played baseball and basketball at the University of Missouri before becoming head basketball coach at Mizzou?

3. What St. Louis Blues great scored six goals against the Philadelphia Flyers on November 7, 1968?

4. Which two members of the University of Missouri basketball team were named All-Americans in 1983?

5. Which University of Missouri wrestler won back-to-back national championships in the 2005–06 and 2006–07 wrestling seasons? (He also became only the second wrestler in history to win two Dan Hodge Trophies as the best collegiate wrestler in the nation.)

6. In what year did Norm Stewart and the University of Missouri men's basketball team complete a perfect 14-0 Big 8 season?

7. The NCAA banned goaltending in 1945 due to the shot-blocking prowess of which St. Louis native, who played for Henry Iba's Oklahoma A&M Aggies (now Oklahoma State)?

8. How many NCAA titles have the Saint Louis University men's soccer team won?

     A. 1   B. 6   C. 10   D. 14

ANSWERS

MISCELLANEOUS

1. Henry Armstrong

2. Norm Stewart

3. Red Berenson

4. Jon Sundvold and Steve Stipanovich

5. Ben Askren

6. 1994

7. Bob Kurland

8. C. 10

PLACES

Missouri has some of the most amazing lakes in all of the United States: Table Rock Lake and Lake Taneycomo in the southwestern corner, Truman Lake in the west central part of the state, Mark Twain Lake in northeast Missouri, and of course, Lake of the Ozarks in central Missouri, just to name a few.

Tens of thousands of people enjoy these lakes every year, but few stop to ponder what lies beneath the surface. Missouri legend details sunken boats, treasures, and catfish the size of whales. But the eerie truth of Missouri's lakes is there are dozens of forgotten cities and homesteads far beneath the water, some still standing to this day.

Table Rock Lake began filling upon completion of the dam in 1958. There were a number of towns and settlements in the low-lying valleys along the White River. One of the most well-known cities to be swamped was the village of Oasis. This small hamlet was situated below the bluffs south of where Big Cedar Lodge stands and north of the present-day Long Creek Bridge. Between two islands, one known as Goat Hill, there is still quite a bit of evidence of the town still standing more than one hundred feet below the surface. Main Street still runs between an old mill, a post office building, and part of the old church. An underwater bridge still stands a few feet way. A half-century in the frigid and dark waters have destroyed much of the wood, but the foundations have persevered.

The old Cedar Valley School is also in Table Rock Lake. It had to be moved a few miles away as the water began filling the winding valley. A settlement known as Ragtown was also swamped. Ragtown was a boomtown near Kimberling City where people came looking for work on the bridge across the White River. This bridge, now known as the "Lost Bridge," still stands more than one hundred feet below the current bridge over Table Rock Lake.

In northeast Missouri, the once flood-prone Salt River was targeted for hydroelectric power by the U.S. Congress. The Clarence Cannon Dam, named after Congressman Clarence Cannon, was dedicated in 1984 and slowly began to fill. Once again, small towns in the valleys became just a memory as the waters filled up what became Mark Twain Lake. One of those forgotten towns is Stoutsville in Monroe County. Victor was another small village with a country store that once stood where water now covers the ground. And the most famous town to be partly flooded was the birthplace of Mark Twain, Florida. Unlike other flooded towns in Missouri, the structures in these small towns were dismantled and sometimes moved to higher ground.

The Lake of the Ozarks has the most cities and settlements that disappeared when the lake filled. In the late 1800s, the banks of the Osage River were a busy trading area. Dotting the river landscape were the towns of Arnold's Mill, old Linn Creek, Nonsuch, Passover, and Zebra. A new Linn Creek was rebuilt once the lake was full and once again became a functioning town alongside the water. These towns were commemorated inside the Willmore Lodge near Bagnell Dam. The lodge was built to host events and administrative events during the building of the dam. Once the project was completed, its five bedrooms were named for the five cities that were swamped.

PLACES

TOWN OR NOT A TOWN?

Ten of the twenty towns listed below are the actual name of a town in Missouri and ten are not. All you have to decide is "town" or "not a town."

1. Bird's Eye
2. Rosebud
3. Jungo
4. Cooter
5. Zalma
6. Oddville
7. Frostproof
8. Peculiar
9. Halfway
10. Velma

11. Hygiene
12. Rugless
13. Novelty
14. Tightwad
15. Amazonia
16. Looneyville
17. Bogard
18. Lupus
19. Pig's Eye
20. Opportunity

ANSWERS

TOWN OR NOT A TOWN?

1. Not a town

2. Town

3. Not a town

4. Town

5. Town

6. Not a town

7. Not a town

8. Town

9. Town

10. Not a town

11. Not a town

12. Not a town

13. Town

14. Town

15. Town

16. Not a town

17. Town

18. Town

19. Not a town

20 Not a town

PLACES

ARCHITECTURE

1. The tallest habitable structure in Missouri is located in which city?

2. Architect Eero Saarinen is famous for designing which iconic Missouri structure?

3. In addition to designing Academic Hall, the first building at the University of Missouri, architect A. Stephen Hills also designed what other Missouri landmark?

4. What well-known American architect designed the Community Christian Church in Kansas City in 1940?

5. The famous Mizzou columns on the quad at the University of Missouri are made from what type of stone?

6. Which Kansas City skyscraper, known for its distinctive Art Deco style, was built in 1931?

7. Built in St. Louis in 1891, what ten-story building was one of the first "skyscrapers" in the world?

8. What type of stone was used to construct the Missouri State Capitol?

9. Built in 1869, which Kansas City bridge was the first to span the Missouri River?

10. Which Jefferson City residence was built on a bluff overlooking the Missouri River in 1871 at a cost of $75,000?

11. What downtown Kansas City building is known for the four lighted pylons extending from its roof?

ANSWERS

ARCHITECTURE

1. Kansas City (One Kansas City Place)

2. The Gateway Arch

3. The State Capitol

4. Frank Lloyd Wright

5. Limestone

6. The Power and Light Building

7. The Wainwright Building

8. Missouri Marble

9. The Hannibal Bridge

10. The Governor's Mansion

11. Bartle Hall

PLACES

BUILDINGS AND LANDMARKS

1. Sitting high on a hill just north of Sedalia, what 12,000 square-foot mansion is available for public tours as a Missouri State Historical Site?

2. In 1892, a fire destroyed Academic Hall at the University of Missouri, leaving what landmark?

3. Construction of Bagnell Dam, which created the Lake of the Ozarks, was completed in which year?

   A. 1915   B. 1920   C. 1931   D. 1935

4. Before moving to the U.S. Supreme Court, the hearings and trials of the landmark *Scott vs. Sandford* case were held in what historic St. Louis building?

5. What once-bustling St. Louis landmark was in operation in its original form from 1894 until 1978? (Since 1985, it has housed a shopping center, restaurants, and hotels.)

6. The ruins of businessman Robert M. Snyder's burned Ozarks mansion are the centerpiece of what Missouri State Park?

7. Which Excelsior Springs resort, long known for its healing mineral water baths, has played host to guests such as Al Capone, Jack Dempsey, and Harry Truman?

8. What is the most visited tourist attraction in Missouri?

ANSWERS

BUILDINGS AND LANDMARKS

1. The Bothwell Lodge

2. The Columns

3. C. 1931

4. The Old Courthouse

5. Union Station

6. Ha Ha Tonka State Park

7. The Elms

8. The Gateway Arch

PLACES

NEIGHBORHOODS

1. Once home to the Kansas City Stockyards, what low-lying section of Kansas City is located near the convergence of the Missouri and Kansas rivers?

2. What is the nickname of the historically Irish neighborhood located near Forest Park in St. Louis?

3. Which south Kansas City neighborhood, located near 75th Street and Wornall Road, bears the last name of the man who founded it in the 1840s?

4. Which St. Louis neighborhood, which surrounds the oldest park west of the Mississippi, is known for its many historic mansions, townhomes, and rowhouses?

5. Which historic neighborhood, located near the Anheuser-Busch Brewery in St. Louis, is known for its popular farmers market?

6. What Kansas City district, named for the intersection of two streets at the heart of the neighborhood, was the hub of African American life in Kansas City in the early twentieth century?

7. Which Kansas City neighborhood near the Plaza is named for the businessman and philanthropist who donated land for the establishment of the University of Missouri–Kansas City?

8. What do Kansas Citians commonly call the suburban areas located north of the Missouri River?

9. What old St. Louis neighborhood, located near the Mississippi River in downtown St. Louis, is known for its active night-life and restaurant scene?

ANSWERS

NEIGHBORHOODS

1. The West Bottoms

2. Dogtown

3. Waldo (David Waldo)

4. Lafayette Square

5. Soulard

6. The 18th and Vine District

7. Volker (William Volker)

8. The Northland

9. Laclede's Landing

PLACES

CITIES AND TOWNS

1. What southeastern Missouri city is named for French trader Jean Girardot?

2. A trading post founded along the Missouri river in 1826 by Joseph Robidoux eventually went on to become what Missouri river city?

3. Which historic resort town in southern Missouri was founded along the White River in 1917?

4. U.S. Presidents Gerald Ford, Ronald Reagan, and George Bush as well as Lech Walesa, Margaret Thatcher, and Mikhail Gorbachev have all spoken at events in what Missouri town?

5. Which north-central Missouri town is known as "the City of Maples"? (There are said to be over 200,000 maple trees within its boundaries.)

6. According the U.S. Census Bureau, in the year 2000, Kansas City, at 313.5 square miles ranked where in land area amongst cities with a population of over 100,000?

7. According to the U.S. Census Bureau, in the year 2007, St. Louis City's population ranked where among the most populous cities in the United States?

    A. 52nd   B. 17th   C. 44th   D. 27th

8. A thriving Presbyterian college was located in which appropriately named, and now unincorporated, town located near Thomas Hill Lake in Macon County from 1853 until 1874?

ANSWERS

CITIES AND TOWNS

1. Cape Girardeau

2. St. Joseph

3. Rockaway Beach

4. Fulton

5. Macon

6. 20th

7. A. 52nd

8. College Mound

PLACES

GEOGRAPHY

1. Approximately how many miles would you drive to get from Watson, in extreme northwest Missouri, to Holland, which is located in extreme southeast Missouri?

    A. 290   B. 440   C. 560   D. 620

2. According to the U.S. Census, the Phelps County town of Edgar Springs holds what unique geographical distinction?

3. The west end of the Katy Trail is located in which Missouri town?

4. Sometimes known as "the Cave State," Missouri has approximately how many surveyed caves?

    A. 1,000   B. 3,000   C. 6,000   D. 10,000

5. What mineral, used in the manufacture of gunpowder, was mined for many years at Meramec Caverns?

6. Which cave, located near Camdenton, was named for a legend involving a Native American wedding that was said to have taken place inside the cave?

7. The east end of the Katy Trail is located in what Missouri city?

8. What is the total length of the Katy Trail?

    A. 167   B. 225   C. 282   D. 312

ANSWERS

GEOGRAPHY

1. C. 550

2. It is the town closest to the mean population center of the United States

3. Clinton

4. C. 6,000

5. Saltpeter

6. Bridal Cave

7. St. Charles

8. B. 225

PLACES

KANSAS CITY OR ST. LOUIS?

Each of the items listed below is associated with one of the two major cities located in Missouri. All you have to do is decide: "Kansas City" or "St. Louis."

1. The Comets

2. The Steamers

3. Burnt ends

4. The Gashouse Gang

5. Toasted ravioli

6. The Jewel Box

7. Benny Moten

8. Buddy Biancalana

9. Carondelet

10. Country Club Plaza

11. Muehlebach

12. Falstaff

13. Bob Forsch

14. WDAF

15. KSDK

16. Signal Hill

ANSWERS

KANSAS CITY OR ST. LOUIS?

1. Kansas City

2. St. Louis

3. Kansas City

4. St. Louis

5. St. Louis

6. St. Louis

7. Kansas City

8. Kansas City

9. St. Louis

10. Kansas City

11. Kansas City

12. St. Louis

13. St. Louis

14. Kansas City

15. St. Louis

16. Kansas City

PLACES

CITIES AND TOWNS

1. The city of Hermann and the surrounding area were largely settled by immigrants from what country?

2. What Missouri town did Martin Warren found in 1856?

3. The town of Smithton, founded in 1819, eventually became which central Missouri city?

4. The Boone's Lick Trail ended in what once-bustling central Missouri town?

5. The American Fur Company's trading center known as Chouteau's Landing eventually became what Missouri city?

6. The name of which city in St. Louis County comes from the French words meaning "broken heart"?

7. An estimated seven million tourists visit which southern Missouri town each year?

8. What Kansas City–area river town was named for prominent resident and abolitionist George S. Park?

9. What Pike County town shares its colorful name with the hometown of its Kentucky founders?

10. Which southwestern Missouri town is named after the mythic "City of Gold" searched for by Spanish conquistadors and explorers?

11. What Kansas City suburb, which is sometimes known by its nickname "happy rock," was founded in 1952?

ANSWERS

CITIES AND TOWNS

1. Germany

2. Warrensburg

3. Columbia

4. Franklin

5. Kansas City

6. Creve Coeur

7. Branson

8. Parkville

9. Bowling Green

10. El Dorado

11. Gladstone

PLACES

COUNTIES

1. Which northeastern Missouri county was named for a famous explorer of the Rocky Mountains?

2. How many Missouri counties were named for persons who were either born in or spent a significant amount of time in Missouri?

    A. 19   B. 28   C. 32   D. 55

3. Which county is named for Missouri's fifth governor? (Kennett is the county seat.)

4. Troy is the county seat of which county that bears the name of, but was not named for, a famous American president?

5. Which county's courthouse in Lexington is believed to be the oldest in continuous use west of the Mississippi River?

6. With a population of 126, what county seat, which shares a name with a famous U.S. president's estate, is the least populated of all the county seats in Missouri? (It is the county seat of Lewis county.)

7. Which northeastern Missouri county bears the name of its founder's European nation of origin?

8. For which U.S. president is Hickory County named?

9. Which county, which is home to Fort Leonard Wood in south-central Missouri, was named for a Polish cavalryman who fought and died in the American Revolution?

ANSWERS

COUNTIES

1. Pike County (Zebulon Pike)

2. B. 28

3. Dunklin County (Daniel Dunklin)

4. Lincoln County (Abraham Lincoln was only ten years old when the county was founded. This county was named for Revolutionary War General Benjamin Lincoln.)

5. Lafayette County

6. Monticello

7. Scotland County

8. Andrew "Old Hickory" Jackson

9. Pulaski County (Kazimierz Pulaski)

PLACES

GEOGRAPHY

1. What is the largest freshwater spring in Missouri?

2. The highest point in Missouri is located at the summit of which Ozark mountain?

3. What geographical feature, whose northern boundary is the Missouri and Osage rivers in Missouri, covers 50,000 square miles in five states?

4. What four Missouri counties share names with U.S. states?

5. Which south-central Missouri town was named for an island nation in the Caribbean?

6. Kansas City sits at the confluence of which two rivers?

7. In 1958, the construction of a dam on the White River in southern Missouri helped to form what lake?

8. What cavern, which is located near Stanton, is the largest commercial cave in the state?

9. Visitors to which Springfield-area cave can tour the cave via motorized trams?

10. What Branson-area amusement park was built around the entrance to Marvel Cave in 1960?

11. What two spring-fed rivers, well-known for great fishing and canoeing, are a part of the Ozark National Scenic Riverways National Park in south-central Missouri?

ANSWERS

GEOGRAPHY

1. Big Spring, in Carter County

2. Taum Sauk Mountain

3. The Ozark Plateau

4. Mississippi, Oregon, Texas, and Washington

5. Cuba

6. The Missouri and the Kansas (Kaw) rivers

7. Table Rock Lake

8. Meramec Caverns

9. Fantastic Caverns

10. Silver Dollar City

11. The Current and Jacks Fork Rivers

PLACES

CITIES AND TOWNS

1. Which southwestern Missouri city is named for a famous South American leader who liberated much of the continent from Spanish rule in the early nineteenth century?

2. What Monroe County town shares a name with a cosmopolitan European capital? (The town was named in honor of the founder's Kentucky hometown, not the European city.)

3. What Missouri town began as a settlement called Boonesborough? (Today it shares its name with a large U.S. state.)

4. What county seat in the green hills of Grundy County is home to North Central Missouri College?

5. What is the county seat of Cape Girardeau County?

6. The Felix Valle House is located in what French-influenced southeastern Missouri town?

7. For whom was the city of St. Louis named?

8. The area around what central Missouri village was called "Pure a Fleche" on early French maps?

9. Which Missouri town was founded in 1836 by members of the German Settlement Society of Philadelphia?

10. Harry Truman moved to what town near Kansas City in 1906 to work on his family's farm?

11. What Morgan County town shares a name, if not a pronunciation, with a famous French palace?

ANSWERS

CITIES AND TOWNS

1. Bolivar (Simon Bolivar)

2. Paris

3. California

4. Trenton

5. Jackson

6. Ste. Genevieve

7. King Louis IX of France

8. Arrow Rock

9. Hermann

10. Grandview

11. Versailles

PLACES

CITIES AND TOWNS

1. What central Missouri town was nicknamed "the Magic City" after a population explosion due to railroad expansion in 1873?

2. What southwest Missouri city is known as "the Queen City of the Ozarks"?

3. What city was once known as "the Paris of the Plains" for its raucous nightlife and entertainment venues?

4. What city was sometimes known as "Mound City" because of the large number of Indian mounds located in its vicinity?

5. Which town, the county seat of Dent County, shares its name with towns, cities, and villages in thirty-five other U.S. states, making it the second most common place-name in the United States?

6. What southeastern Missouri lead-mining town was named after a mining city in Bolivia?

7. Which Carroll County town is the self-proclaimed "Soybean Capital of the World" and holds a Soybean Festival every August?

8. Both the coldest and warmest temperatures in the state of Missouri were recorded in which south-central Missouri town located near Truman Lake?

9. What unincorporated town near Maryville has been home to a Roman Catholic monastery since 1881?

ANSWERS

CITIES AND TOWNS

1. Moberly

2. Springfield

3. Kansas City

4. St. Louis

5. Salem

6. Potosi

7. Norborne

8. Warsaw

9. Conception (Conception Abbey)

PLACES

COUNTIES

1. How many counties are in Missouri?

    A. 99   B. 108   C. 114   D. 121

2. More than twenty Missouri's counties were named for participants of what war?

3. Which northwestern Missouri county is Missouri's smallest by both land area (266 square miles) and population (2,382)?

4. Which county, named after a large U.S. state, at 1,179 square miles is the largest in Missouri by land area?

5. What is the most populous county in Missouri?

6. Which county, whose seat is Farmington, was named for St. Francis of Assisi?

7. Which suburban St. Louis county sits in an area that was called "San Carlos" by early Spanish settlers?

8. What is the name of the extreme northeastern county in Missouri? (It was named for a famous explorer and governor of the Missouri Territory.)

9. What is the only Missouri county named for a type of tree?

10. Which west-central Missouri county was named for a Frenchman who fought against the British as a general in the American Revolutionary War?

11. In what year did St. Louis City split from St. Louis County?

ANSWERS

COUNTIES

1. C. 114

2. The American Revolutionary War

3. Worth County

4. Texas County

5. St. Louis County

6. St. Francois County

7. St. Charles County

8. Clark County (William Clark)

9. Cedar County (Hickory County is named for Andrew Jackson)

10. Lafayette County (Marquis de Lafayette)

11. 1876 (known as the Great Divorce of 1876)

PLACES

GEOGRAPHY

1. What river was impounded in 1920 to form the Lake of the Ozarks?

2. According to the U.S. Census Bureau in 2007, Kansas City's population ranks where among the most populous cities in the United States?

    A. 18th   B. 60th   C. 39th   D. 25th

3. Missouri leads the nation in supplying what metal? (It is mined mostly in southeastern Missouri.)

4. Approximately how many square miles does the state of Missouri occupy?

    A. 40,000   B. 55,000   C. 70,000   D. 85,000

5. The geographical center of Missouri is located approximately twenty miles southwest of which Missouri city?

6. The region along the Missouri River in central Missouri that includes Audrain, Callaway, Boone, and Howard counties is sometimes known by what nickname because of the culture and lifestyle that its many Southern-born settlers brought to the area in the early nineteenth century?

7. What is the name of Missouri's 1.5 million–acre national forest?

8. What are the eight states that share borders with the state of Missouri?

ANSWERS

GEOGRAPHY

1. The Osage River

2. C. 39th

3. Lead

4. C. 70,000

5. Jefferson City

6. Little Dixie

7. Mark Twain National Forest

8. Nebraska, Iowa, Illinois, Kentucky, Tennessee, Arkansas, Oklahoma and Kansas

PEOPLE

Walter Elias Disney has changed the way the world is entertained perhaps more than anyone in history. The technology he invented, the films he produced, and the theme parks he designed continue to entertain hundreds of millions of people every year around the globe. And his dream to change the world all began in small-town Missouri.

Walt Disney was born in Chicago, but he moved with his family to Marceline, Missouri as a boy. He grew up in a poor household with five siblings and ended up moving to Kansas City when his father lost the family farm and was forced to move. In Kansas City, he attended art school and eventually began producing short animated commercials.

In the early 1920s, Disney realized if he wanted to reach the top of the film industry, he had to move to California. He made a name for himself, and a fortune, in Los Angeles by creating some of the most memorable animated characters of all time, including Cinderella, Dumbo, Bambi, and of course, Mickey Mouse.

Despite his success in film production and animation, he often said he was most proud of his theme park, Disneyland in California, and his plans for a similar park in Florida. The fact that Disney almost built a theme park in downtown St. Louis is largely lost to history. He had a vision for a theme park that would stretch from north to south along the Mississippi Riverfront. At the time he was entertaining the idea of building the park, the most famous monument of Missouri was also in the planning stages. His Americana-themed park would tie in nicely with the Gateway Arch. He knew the incredible potential of that stretch of land. Not only would it soon contain the Arch, but it also would be at the crossroads of America. Three major interstates were to cross just south of where he planned to build the theme park.

At the same time he was planning the St. Louis park, he was also looking toward central Florida. The small town of Orlando, Florida, had a population of less than 50,000 in the mid-1960s, with year-round warm temperatures and plenty of land for development. Orange farmers were abandoning their land as newer technology made it easier to harvest more oranges from less land. So Disney quietly began buying thousands and thousands of acres of swampland, often in different names to not arouse suspicions, where he would eventually build his second theme park. It was for this reason, along with opposition from some St. Louis city leaders that he abandoned his plans in St. Louis and decided to solely focus his efforts on central Florida.

Although a Disney park didn't actually come to Missouri, millions of tourists who go to Disney every year do get to take a trip through the Show Me State. Downtown Disney, as it is called in his theme parks, was in fact based on Marceline, Missouri. His fond memories of small-town Missouri have been immortalized for all to enjoy. Sadly, Walt Disney died before his Florida dream came true. He passed away in 1966, five years before Walt Disney World in Orlando, Florida, was completed.

PEOPLE

GENERAL

1. Magazine publisher Condé Nast earned a law degree at which Missouri university in 1897?

2. Missourian Julia Boggs Dent was the wife of which famous American soldier and 18th president of the United States?

3. William Clark, Thomas Hart Benton, Sterling Price, William Burroughs, and Adolphus Busch are all buried in which St. Louis cemetery?

4. Marlin Perkins, the host of *Mutual of Omaha's Wild Kingdom*, was born in what southwestern Missouri town in 1905?

5. Conservative radio star Rush Limbaugh was born in which southeastern Missouri city?

6. For whom did poet Eugene Field's father, Roswell Field, represent as an attorney in a landmark St. Louis court case in the late 1840s?

7. What Independence-born beauty was Fred Astaire's dance partner in a series of wildly popular 1930s musicals?

8. Which legendary Confederate Civil War general was stationed in St. Louis in 1837 as the supervisor of navigational works on the Mississippi River for the U.S. Army?

9. Saxophonist and St. Joseph native Coleman Hawkins was a well-known musician in what genre of music?

ANSWERS

GENERAL

1. Washington University

2. Ulysses S. Grant

3. Bellefontaine Cemetery

4. Carthage

5. Cape Girardeau

6. Dred Scott

7. Ginger Rogers

8. Robert E. Lee

9. Jazz

PEOPLE

BORN IN MISSOURI?

Eight of the people listed below were born in Missouri and eight of them were not. All you have to do is decide: "born in Missouri" or "not born in Missouri."

1. Langston Hughes

2. Fred Astaire

3. Ginger Rogers

4. Eberhard Anheuser

5. Nick Nolte

6. Don Cheadle

7. Jane Wyman

8. Jayne Mansfield

9. Dennis Hopper

10. Hunter S. Thompson

11. Marshall Mathers (Eminem)

12 Douglas MacArthur

13. John Goodman

14. Omar Bradley

15. Bob Newhart

16. Dick Van Dyke

ANSWERS

BORN IN MISSOURI?

1. Born in Missouri (Joplin)

2. Not born in Missouri (Omaha, Nebraska)

3. Born in Missouri (Independence)

4. Not born in Missouri (Germany)

5. Not born in Missouri (Omaha, Nebraska)

6. Born in Missouri (Kansas City)

7. Born in Missouri (St. Joseph)

8. Not born in Missouri (Bryn Mawr, Pennsylvania)

9. Not born in Missouri (Dodge City, Kansas)

10. Not born in Missouri (Louisville, Kentucky)

11. Born in Missouri (St. Joseph)

12. Not born in Missouri (Little Rock, Arkansas)

13. Born in Missouri (Affton)

14. Born in Missouri (Clark)

15. Not born in Missouri (Oak Park, Illinois)

16. Born in Missouri (West Plains)

PEOPLE

GENERAL

1. Missouri Botanical Garden founder Henry Shaw made his fortune in what retail business?

2. Who did Bess Wallace marry on June 28, 1919?

3. What Missouri-born writer was hired by *The Sacramento Union* newspaper to write about his experiences while traveling in Hawaii in 1866?

4. Kansas City's downtown convention center is named for which mayor of Kansas City who served from 1955 to 1963?

5. Three Missouri S&T (University of Missouri–Rolla) graduates—Sandra Magnus, Janet Kavandi, and Thomas Akers—have held what high-flying job?

6. What political office did Harry Truman hold just before being elected to the U.S. Senate in 1934?

7. What type of doll, very popular in the early twentieth century, was based on the drawings of Missouri resident Rose O'Neill?

8. What influential Texan, for whom the capital of Texas is named, moved to Missouri at the age of four with his father Moses?

9. What successful St. Louis stockbroker helped defend St. Louis from Confederate forces during the Civil War as a general in the Missouri Militia?

10. Hannibal native William Lear, who founded the Lear Jet Corporation, helped develop what popular audio device of the 1960s and 1970s?

ANSWERS

GENERAL

1. Hardware

2. Harry Truman

3. Samuel Clemens (Mark Twain)

4. Harold Roe Bartle

5. Astronaut

6. Presiding Judge of Jackson County

7. Kewpie Dolls

8. Stephen F. Austin

9. Albert Gallatin (A. G.) Edwards

10. The 8-track tape

PEOPLE

QUOTES

Each of the quotes below was spoken by a famous Missourian.
Name the Missourian responsible for each one.

1. "The buck stops here."

2. "All our dreams can come true, if we have the courage to
   pursue them."

3. "Help control the pet population, have your pets spayed or
   neutered."

4. "A man is never more truthful than when he acknowledges
   himself a liar."

5. "Ninety percent of this game is mental and the other half is
   physical."

6. "Health food makes me sick."

7. "Holy cow!"

8, "This is the big one! You hear that Elizabeth? I'm coming to
   join you honey!"

9. "We'll wait here while Jim . . ."

10. "Can't anybody here play this game?"

11. "Education is the key to unlock the golden door of freedom."

12. "Capital isn't scarce, vision is."

ANSWERS

QUOTES

1. Harry S. Truman

2. Walt Disney

3. Bob Barker

4. Mark Twain

5. Yogi Berra

6. Calvin Trillin

7. Harry Caray

8. Redd Foxx

9. Marlin Perkins

10. Casey Stengel

11. George Washington Carver

12. Sam Walton

PEOPLE

HARRY S. TRUMAN

1. Harry Truman was born in 1884 in which southwest Missouri town?

2. Truman attended, but did not graduate from, which Missouri university?

3. What occupation did Truman take up in Kansas City following his return from service in World War I?

4. Truman moved from the position of vice president to president of the United States on April 12, 1945, due to the death of which president?

5. How many days did Truman hold the office of vice president of the United States?

     A. 70   B. 82   C. 112   D. 365

6. What did the headline of *The Chicago Tribune* incorrectly read in the famous photo of Truman after his presidential re-election in 1948?

7. How many children did Harry and Bess Truman have?

8. During the winter months of his presidency, Truman spent a great deal of time at his "Little White House," which was located in what Florida city?

9. Gunmen from what Caribbean island attempted to assassinate Truman at the Blair House in Washington, D.C., in 1950?

ANSWERS

HARRY S. TRUMAN

1. Lamar

2. The Kansas City School of Law (UMKC)

3. Haberdasher

4. Franklin D. Roosevelt

5. B. 82

6. "Dewey Defeats Truman"

7. One, a daughter, Mary Margaret Truman

8. Key West

9. Puerto Rico

PEOPLE

GENERAL

1. A series of murals by what well-known Missouri artist decorate many of the walls at the Missouri State Capitol in Jefferson City?

2. What legendary photographer, who was known for his Farm Security Administration (FSA) work and his collaboration with James Agee on the book *Let Us Now Praise Famous Men*, was born in St. Louis in 1903?

3. Who founded the Western Auto Company in Kansas City in 1909, as well as the Malibu, California, university that bears his name?

4. Although the validity of the claim is debated, Missourian David Rice Atchison is said to have held what political office for one day in 1849?

5. What former Civil War Bushwhacker from Kearney became a folk legend and the most famous outlaw in American History after he and his gang committed numerous bank and train robberies throughout the Midwest in the 1860s and 1870s?

6. Bethany native Frank Buckles gained fame in 2007 as the last known surviving veteran of what war?

7. William Rockhill Nelson founded what influential Missouri newspaper in 1880?

8. In 1855, armed bands of Missourians, led by David Rice Atchison and Claiborne Fox Jackson, forced officials of which neighboring state to let them vote in their state's legislative elections?

9. What famous survivor of the *Titanic* was born Margaret Tobin in Hannibal in 1867?

ANSWERS

GENERAL

1. Thomas Hart Benton

2. Walker Evans

3. George Pepperdine

4. President of the United States

5. Jesse James

6. World War I

7. *Kansas City Star*

8. Kansas

9. "The Unsinkable" Molly Brown

PEOPLE

GENERAL

1. The father and namesake of what famously reclusive billionaire aviator, director, and movie producer was born in Lancaster in 1869?

2. Arrow Rock's John Sappington first introduced the use of Quinine in pill form in treating what insect-borne illness?

3. What Maryville native wrote the bestseller *How to Win Friends and Influence People*?

4. Missouri Senator George Graham Vest is known for acting as an attorney in the famous Warrensburg court case involving a dog known by what name?

5. Which politician, whose namesake county is home to the Missouri State Fair, died along with opponent Thomas Biddle from wounds received during a duel in 1831?

6. Which Liberty resident, for whom a county in Kansas is named, was a soldier and politician who participated in the Mexican-American War and the "Mormon Wars" of Missouri?

7. Comedian and actor David Koechner, known for his role as sportscaster Champ Kind in the 2004 comedy *Anchorman, The Legend of Ron Burgandy*, hails from what central Missouri town?

8. Las Vegas businessman Jay Sarno, who built both the Circus Circus and Caesar's Palace casinos, was a native of what Missouri river city?

9. What Mill Spring native, who went on to found a magazine publishing empire, advocated bodybuilding, exercise, and nutrition as a way of life with his 1899 magazine Physical Culture?

ANSWERS

GENERAL

1. Howard Hughes

2. Malaria

3. Dale Carnegie

4. Old Drum

5. Spencer Pettis

6. Alexander Doniphan

7. Tipton

8. St. Joseph

9. Bernarr Macfadden

PEOPLE

GENERAL

1. How did future Missouri Governor John S. Marmaduke kill fellow Confederate Army General Lucius Walker in 1863?

2. *St. Louis Observer* publisher Elijah Lovejoy was driven from St. Louis and later killed by a mob in Alton, Illinois, because of his support of what nineteenth-century movement?

3. Who worked as a newspaper reporter in St. Louis before famously catching up with Dr. Livingstone in Africa in 1871?

4. Known as "the most trusted man in America" what journalist and anchorman of the CBS Evening News was born in St. Joseph in 1916?

5. Born in Sumner in 1905, what long-time Arkansas senator established the prestigious international scholarship which bears his name in 1945?

6. John H. Lathrop was the first president of which Missouri institution of higher learning?

7. A NASA space telescope bears the name of what great astronomer who was born in Marshfield in 1889?

8. Which great Missourian, who represented Missouri as a U.S. senator from 1821 to 1851, shares a name with his artistic great-nephew?

9. What Kansas City park, located at 51st and Wornall Road, takes its name from a businessman who built a fortune manufacturing crackers in the late nineteenth century?

ANSWERS

GENERAL

1. He shot him in a duel

2. Abolitionism

3. Henry M. Stanley

4. Walter Cronkite

5. J. William Fulbright

6. The University of Missouri

7. Edwin Hubble

8. Thomas Hart Benton

9. Loose Park (Jacob Loose)

PEOPLE

GENERAL

1. Who, after being born into slavery near Diamond Grove in 1864, went on to teach at the Tuskegee Institute in Alabama where his agricultural innovations helped change the world?

2. What cartoonist grew up in Kansas City and attended the University of Missouri before joining the military and later creating the comic strip *Beetle Bailey?*

3. Who opened a commercial art studio in downtown Kansas City in 1920 after returning from service with the Red Cross in Europe?

4. In 1955, the Sedalia Air Force Base was renamed in honor of what Longwood-born pilot who was killed during the attack on Pearl Harbor in 1941?

5. Born in St. Louis in 1906, what internationally famous beauty rose to prominence as a dancer, singer, and actress in Paris, France, in the 1920s and 1930s?

6. Comic, civil rights activist, and author Dick Gregory was born in what Missouri city in 1932?

7. Before he became the governor of Missouri, John S. Phelps successfully defended which Wild West legend in a trial over the shooting death of a Springfield man in 1865?

8. What Missouri politician, along with partner Eddie Jacobsen, operated a men's clothing store at 104 W. 12th Street in Kansas City from 1919 to 1922?

ANSWERS

GENERAL

1. George Washington Carver

2. Mort Walker

3. Walt Disney

4. George Whiteman

5. Josephine Baker

6. St. Louis

7. Wild Bill Hickok

8. Harry S. Truman

ARTS

Music has always been a big part of Missouri's heritage. The state is known for its jazz and blues, waltzes, and of course, bluegrass. Contemporary music, though, is having a huge impact on people around the world. As a matter of fact, Missouri natives have generated an impressive, and possibly even surprising, amount of No. 1 hits.

Country music is a staple of many towns. But few people realize that the "dean" of the Grand Ole Opry in Nashville, Tennessee, is a man from southern Missouri. Porter Wagoner spent fifty years at the Opry, recording songs with the biggest names in music. He had eighty-one songs hit the country music charts, including three No. 1 hits. His biggest success came with the twenty-one-year run of *The Porter Wagoner Show*, which was seen by millions of television viewers every week. He also won numerous Vocal Duet of the Year Awards alongside his regular singing partner, Dolly Parton.

Another country superstar hails from New Franklin. Sara Evans rose to fame in the 1990s and hit No. 1 with "Born to Fly." That song also won the honor of Video of the Year by the Country Music Association. "Born to Fly" was just the first of several chart-topping hits for the country crooner. She went on to win the prestigious award of Female Vocalist of the Year by Radio and Records and Top Female Vocalist by the Academy of Country Music in 2006.

The woman once said to have the sexiest lips in Rock and Roll, Sheryl Crow, also hails from Missouri. Crow grew up in the bootheel town of Kennett. She graduated from Mizzou and became a teacher in the St. Louis area. But her talents eventually led her back to a career in music that rivals any star over the era. Sheryl first hit No. 1 on the Billboard charts with "All I Wanna Do" in 1994. She had numerous Top 10 hits before landing on top of the charts once again in 2002 with "Soak Up the Sun." The southeast Missouri native has also won "Best Female Rock Vocal Performance" by the National Academy of Recording Arts and Sciences, numerous times. Interestingly, her amazing solo success came after several years of backup singing for arguably the biggest musical star in history, Michael Jackson.

The St. Louis rap scene burst onto the radar in 2000 with a young rapper named Nelly. Nelly shot straight to No. 1 and captivated the country in a way not often seen. The album, *Country Grammar*, generated four hits, including "Ride Wit Me." *Country Grammar* shot to No. 1 on the album charts and sold over 9 million copies, certifying it as nine times platinum.

In modern Jazz, two of the biggest names in the industry also hail from Missouri. Pat Metheny grew up in the Kansas City suburb of Lee's Summit and went on to form the Pat Metheny Group. He was such a prolific performer that when he dropped out of the University of Miami, he was immediately offered a teaching position at the school. For more than three decades, he has continued to have chart-topping songs.

Jazz saxophonist David Sanborn from the St. Louis suburb of Kirkwood, is also a standout artist of our era. He has had numerous chart toppers, but is likely best known for the theme to *L.A. Law*, which he wrote and performed.

ARTS

LITERATURE

1. What great American writer spent six months as an eighteen-year-old cub reporter at the *Kansas City Star* before volunteering with the Red Cross ambulance service in World War I?

2. Novelist Kate Chopin, whose acclaimed book *The Awakening* was published in 1899, was born in which Missouri city?

3. Although Mark Twain grew up in Hannibal he was actually born in what tiny Missouri town?

4. What St. Louis–born journalist and poet penned a poem about a scenic stretch of road in St. Joseph titled *Lover's Lane St. Jo*?

5. Which African-American literary icon and catalyst of the Harlem Renaissance was born in Joplin in 1902? (He spent most of his childhood in Lawrence, Kansas.)

6. Which beat generation writer and author of *Naked Lunch* was born in St. Louis in 1914?

7. Playwright Thomas Lanier Williams II, who spent his childhood in St. Louis and attended both the University of Missouri and Washington University, is better known by what famous moniker?

8. Author Evan Connell, famous for his novels *Mr. Bridge* and *Mrs. Bridge*, was born in which Missouri city?

9. The Center for Faulkner Studies, a collection of materials and information concerning author William Faulkner, is located at what Missouri university?

ANSWERS

LITERATURE

1. Ernest Hemingway

2. St. Louis

3. Florida

4. Eugene Field

5. Langston Hughes

6. William Burroughs

7. Tennessee Williams

8. Kansas City

9. Southeast Missouri State University

ARTS

MUSIC

1. What popular song is based on a murder in St. Louis in 1899 in which a woman named Frankie Baker killed her boyfriend as revenge for his infidelity?

2. St. Louis musician Johnny Johnson was the inspiration for what famous Chuck Berry hit?

3. What ragtime and jazz great, who shares his last name with a famous pioneer, was born in Miami, Missouri, and later lived in both Warrensburg and Columbia?

4. The home of what legendary ragtime musician and composer was located on Delmar Boulevard in St. Louis? (It is now a Missouri State Historic Site.)

5. Saxophone legend David Sandborn hails from which St. Louis suburb?

6. Mississippi John Hurt, Bob Dylan, Tina Turner, and Wilson Pickett have all recorded versions of what song based on an 1895 murder in St. Louis?

7. Composer and pianist Burt Bacharach was born in which Missouri city in 1928?

8. Washington, Missouri, was once home to the premier manufacturer of what stringed musical instrument?

9. St. Louis–born Michael McDonald rose to musical prominence after joining what 1970s rock band?

10. The Max Weinberg 7's trumpet player, Mark Pender, was born and raised in what Missouri city?

ANSWERS

MUSIC

1. *Frankie and Johnny*

2. *Johnny B. Goode*

3. John "Blind" Boone

4. Scott Joplin

5. Kirkwood

6. *Stagger Lee*

7. Kansas City

8. The Zither

9. The Doobie Brothers

10. Kansas City

ARTS

LITERATURE

1. What St. Louis–born novelist rose to popularity in the early twentieth century with novels such as *The Crisis* and *Richard Carvel*? (Despite his success he is often confused with a famous British Prime Minister of the same name.)

2. Despite being an accomplished journalist, novelist, and war correspondent, St. Louis–born Martha Gellhorn is most often remembered as the third wife of what famous novelist?

3. Parts of James Ellroy's novel *Killshot* were set in which southeastern Missouri city?

4. What 1907 novel by Harold Bell Wright is re-enacted nightly from May to September at an outdoor theater near Branson?

5. Boonville native Charles Van Ravenswaay, as the state supervisor of the Missouri Writer's Project, spearheaded the completion of what comprehensive guidebook first published in 1941?

6. Novelist Rupert Hughes, the uncle of billionaire Howard Hughes, was born in what northeastern Missouri town?

7. What Henry Bellamann novel, which was made into a motion picture starring Ronald Reagan in 1942, deals with life in Bellamann's native Fulton?

8. Missourian William Least Heat-Moon is the author of what classic travel book about his adventures roaming the back roads of America in 1978?

ANSWERS

LITERATURE

1. Winston Churchill

2. Ernest Hemingway

3. Cape Girardeau

4. *The Shepherd of the Hills*

5. *Missouri: A Guide to the 'Show Me' State* (The WPA guide to Missouri)

6. Lancaster

7. *King's Row*

8. *Blue Highways*

ARTS

TELEVISION AND THE MOVIES

1. What St. Louis–born actor, known for roles in numerous horror films, famously narrated Michael Jackson's *Thriller* in 1983?

2. What Missouri television station is used to train journalism students preparing to enter the television industry?

3. An acclaimed 2002 documentary by Kansas Citian Hali Lee documented the lives of a diverse set of Kansas City teenagers in the days leading up to what major high school social event?

4. The 1972 movie *Kansas City Bomber*, starring Raquel Welch, was about what theatrically violent sport?

5. What St. Louis–born actor won a Best Supporting Actor Oscar in 1989 for his role in *A Fish Called Wanda*?

6. What 1976 movie starred Clint Eastwood as a Missouri farmer who joins with a band of Bushwhackers in order to exact revenge against the Kansas Jayhawkers who killed his family?

7. Which actor, who famously portrayed General George Patton in the 1970 movie *Patton*, was a student at the University of Missouri in the 1950s?

8. From 1993 to 1996, what former *Night Court* actor had his own NBC sitcom set in a St. Louis bus depot?

9. The 1989 movie *Road House*, starring Patrick Swayze, was set in what southwestern Missouri town?

10. What 1959 heist film, based on an actual crime in St. Louis, starred one-time Missourian Steve McQueen?

ANSWERS

TELEVISION AND THE MOVIES

1. Vincent Price

2. KOMU-TV (Columbia)

3. The Prom (*Prom Night in Kansas City*)

4. Roller Derby

5. Kevin Kline

6. *The Outlaw Josey Wales*

7. George C. Scott

8. John Larroquette

9. Jasper

10. *The Great St. Louis Bank Robbery*

ARTS

LITERATURE

1. What St. Louis–born poet is memorialized, along with the likes of William Shakespeare and Dylan Thomas, at the famed "Poets' Corner" of London's Westminster Abbey?

2. Jack Conroy, whose writings about the American working-class include the novel *The Disinherited*, was born in a coal mining camp known as "the Monkey's Nest" near what central Missouri town?

3. Laura Ingalls Wilder wrote her *Little House* series of books while living at her family's Rocky Ridge Farm near what southwest Missouri town?

4. What Kansas City–born novelist and long-time writer at *The New Yorker* once called Arthur Bryant's Barbeque in Kansas City "the best restaurant in the world"?

5. St. Louis–born Sally Benson's short story about the 1904 World's Fair was made into what classic movie musical of the same name starring Judy Garland?

6. What author of *Omensetter's Luck* and *The Tunnel* headed up the International Writer's Center at Washington University in St. Louis?

7. The prestigious annual prize for the best American journalism, literature, music, and drama was established in 1917 by what powerful St. Louis newspaper publisher?

8. What well-known writer and activist from St. Louis rose to fame with the publication of her autobiographical novel *I Know Why the Caged Bird Sings* in 1969?

ANSWERS

LITERATURE

1. T. S. Eliot

2. Moberly

3. Mansfield

4. Calvin Trillin

5. *Meet Me in St. Louis*

6. William Gass

7. Joseph Pulitzer

8. Maya Angelou

ARTS

TELEVISION AND THE MOVIES

1. St. Louis native Jenna Fischer, known for the role of "Pam" on the comedy series *The Office*, attended which northeastern Missouri college?

2. Actress Kathleen Turner was born in which Missouri city?

3. What actor, who is best known for the role of "Norm" on the sitcom *Cheers*, graduated from Rockhurst University in Kansas City?

4. Which Independence native was the producer and writer of the comedy series *The Beverly Hillbillies?*

5. What legendary comedian and star of a popular 1970s network comedy series was born John Elroy Sanford in St. Louis in 1922?

6. An iconic photograph of which St. Louis–born actress in a bikini made her the most popular "pin-up girl" among American servicemen in World War II?

7. Which legendary director, whose films include *The Maltese Falcon, Night of the Iguana, The Misfits, Casino Royale,* and *Prizzi's Honor* was born in Nevada, Missouri, in 1906?

8. Robert Guillaume, best known for the role of "Benson," was born in which Missouri city?

9. Robert Altman wrote and directed what appropriately titled movie about his hometown in 1996?

10. Much of the 1973 movie *Tom Sawyer* was filmed in which central Missouri village?

ANSWERS

TELEVISION AND THE MOVIES

1. Truman State University (Northeast Missouri State)

2. Springfield

3. George Wendt

4. Paul Henning

5. Redd Foxx

6. Betty Grable

7. John Huston

8. St. Louis

9. *Kansas City*

10. Arrow Rock

ARTS

LITERATURE

1. What great English writer visited St. Louis during his 1842 tour of the United States?

2. Which St. Louis–born author's first novel, *Junkie*, was written under the pen name "William Lee"?

3. Who is the only Missourian to win the Nobel Prize for Literature?

4. What famous cookbook has sold over 18 million copies since it was first self-published by St. Louis's Irma Rombauer in 1931?

5. What famous aviator, often associated with St. Louis, won a Pulitzer Prize for his autobiography in 1954?

6. Influential science fiction writer Robert Heinlein, author of *Starship Troopers* and *Stranger in a Strange Land*, was born in Butler in 1907 but grew up in what Missouri city?

7. Which St. Louis–born author's first book was the self-published novel *At Fault?*

8. Ernest Hemingway was once quoted as saying that all of American literature comes from which Mark Twain novel?

9. Kirkwood-born author Josephine Johnson won what prize, at the age of twenty-four, for her first novel *Now in November?*

10. Homer Croy's 1922 novel *West of the Water Tower* was an account of life in what northwest Missouri college town?

ANSWERS

LITERATURE

1. Charles Dickens

2. William Burroughs

3. T. S. Eliot

4. *The Joy of Cooking*

5. Charles Lindbergh

6. Kansas City

7. Kate Chopin

8. *Huckleberry Finn*

9. The Pulitzer Prize

10. Maryville

ARTS

MUSIC

1. Number one hits like Born to Fly and Suds in the Bucket helped propel what New Franklin native to country music stardom?

2. What tune became Missouri's official state song in 1949?

3. Which rapper, born Cornell Haynes Jr., put St. Louis hip-hop on the map with his 2000 album *Country Grammar?*

4. Which legendary British rock band took a mini-vacation from their 1964 American tour at airline owner Reed Pigman's ranch near Alton?

5. What band, known for hits like *Jackie Blue* and *If You Wanna Get to Heaven*, was formed in Springfield in the 1970s?

6. What popular song with a Missouri connection was written by "the Father of the Blues," W. C. Handy, in 1912?

7. What music legend, born Anna Mae Bullock in 1939, began her music career by singing with her future husband in St. Louis after moving to the area from Tennessee as a sixteen year old?

8. In 1991, which heavy metal front-man incited a riot at a St. Louis amphitheater by jumping into the crowd to stop an audience member from taping his band's performance?

9. What bandleader and his famous orchestra began performing in Kansas City jazz clubs in the 1930s?

10. What famed opera singer made his international debut at William Jewell College in Liberty in 1973?

ANSWERS

MUSIC

1. Sara Evans

2. *The Missouri Waltz*

3. Nelly

4. The Beatles

5. The Ozark Mountain Daredevils

6. *St. Louis Blues*

7. Tina Turner

8. Axl Rose

9. William "Count" Basie

10. Luciano Pavarotti

ARTS

LITERATURE

1. What central Missouri town is mentioned on the second page of Jack Kerouac's 1957 novel *On the Road?*

2. Which novelist, who wrote *Grendel, The Sunlight Dialogues,* and *On Becoming a Novelist,* graduated from Washington University in St. Louis in 1955?

3. Poet Sara Teasdale was born in which Missouri city in 1884?

4. Who is the Webster Groves–reared author of the novels *The Twenty-Seventh City* and *The Corrections?*

5. St. Louis native and Washington University graduate A. E. Hotchner is best known for writing the 1966 biography of which great American writer?

6. *The Innocents Abroad,* published in 1869, was the first book by which Missouri author?

7. Which Maryville native's book, *How to Win Friends and Influence People,* has sold over 10 million copies since it was first published in 1936?

8. In the Ernest Hemingway novel *The Sun Also Rises,* protagonist Jake Barnes claims that he is from which Missouri city?

9. Missourian Daniel Woodrell's 1987 novel *Woe to Live On,* about the border war between Missouri Bushwhackers and Kansas Jay-hawkers, was the basis for what 1999 movie directed by Ang Lee?

10. Who is Tom Sawyer's "love interest" in Mark Twain's 1876 novel *The Adventures of Tom Sawyer?*

ANSWERS

LITERATURE

1. Boonville

2. John Gardner

3. St. Louis

4. Jonathan Franzen

5. Ernest Hemingway

6. Mark Twain

7. Dale Carnegie

8. Kansas City

9. *Ride With the Devil*

10. Becky Thatcher

BUSINESS & POLITICS

V ery few states can lay claim to the number of "legendary" business names that are known around the globe. This mid-sized state in the middle of the country has more than its fair share of companies that have changed the way the world does business. There are a number of theories about why the Show Me State has such a large list of well-known businesses. Perhaps the best explanation is simply that success takes courage and determination; two characteristics Missourians have plenty of.

One of the best examples of this type of work ethic is James Cash Penney. He grew up in the small town of Hamilton. Penney was forced to buy his own clothing as a child, because his father wanted him to learn the value of hard work and discipline. His father also instilled in him the "Golden Rule": "Do unto others and you would have done unto you." This value permeated life at home and came to be the underlying belief for his chain of stores long after he was gone. As an added piece of irony, the first real job James had in the retail word was for a chain of stores in Colorado called "Golden Rule." Penney eventually opened his own stores called J. C. Penney in 1908, quickly growing into a nationally recognized chain of department stores. Interestingly enough, he refused to accept credit and only took cash because he thought it was in the best interest of the customers. He built a business based on superior value and good customer service, all the while putting employees and customers first.

Another company whose founder grew up in mid-Missouri is the granddaddy retailer of them all. The most successful retail company of all time is of course Wal-Mart. The idea for the mega-stores were hatched right here in Missouri as legendary businessman Sam Walton looked for ways to give people good products at low prices. Walton grew up in Columbia and attended the University of Missouri where he worked odd jobs to pay for school. The lessons he learned about the value of a dollar from his early years of hard work were a driving force behind the success of the business. The first stores actually opened in Arkansas but spread across Missouri in the early years. He went from a poor young man to the richest man of all time in the course of his lifetime due to looking out for his customers.

There are far more amazing business success stories from right here in Missouri, many that people don't realize got their start in the Show Me State. Anheuser-Busch began in St. Louis thanks to the legendary businessman Adolphus Busch. Americans exchange Christmas presents thanks in part to the Hall brothers, who invented wrapping paper and founded Hallmark Cards in Kansas City. Millions of tax returns are filed every year thanks to Henry Bloch of Kansas City, who made tax preparation available to the masses with his firm, H&R Block. Auto parts stores stretch from coast to coast with the name O'Reilly emblazoned across the sign thanks to the vision of the O'Reilly family in Springfield. Business jets are often called Lear Jets, despite the fact that Lear is a particular brand based on jets invented by Bill Lear. Lear, born in Hannibal, also invented the 8-track tape player.

As the great sales trainer Dale Carnegie (also from Missouri) is quoted as saying, "Our life is what our thoughts make it." And that is certainly true in Missouri. There have always been big dreams in the Show Me State. When those dreams are coupled with Missouri's reputation for stubborn resilience and hard work, success is sure to come. In fact, in the world of business, that's the only path to success.

BUSINESS & POLITICS

1. How many congressmen represent Missouri in the U.S. House of Representatives?

2. Alexander McNair holds what distinction among Missouri's governors?

3. St. Louis native and Washington University graduate George Herbert Walker is the grandfather of which U.S. president?

4. Associate Justice of the Supreme Court Charles Whittaker received his law degree from what Missouri school?

5. How many judges typically make up the Missouri Supreme Court?

6. Harry Truman was the only U.S. president of the twentieth century to have not earned what?

7. Former President of Nicaragua Enrique Balanos graduated from which Catholic university in Missouri?

8. How many electoral votes are allotted to Missouri in presidential elections?

    A. 11   B. 4   C. 14   D. 20

9. Missourian Edward Bates served as U.S. attorney general under which famous nineteenth-century American president?

10. Much like a state-level Secret Service, a division of what Missouri agency is responsible for the transportation, security, and protection of Missouri's governor?

ANSWERS

BUSINESS & POLITICS

1. Nine

2. He was the first

3. George Herbert Walker Bush

4. The Kansas City School of Law (UMKC)

5. Seven

6. Earned a college degree

7. Saint Louis University

8. A. 11

9. Abraham Lincoln

10. The Missouri State Highway Patrol

BUSINESS & POLITICS

1. The 1976 Republican National Convention was held in what Kansas City building?

2. A boulevard near the County Club Plaza in Kansas City bears the name of which mayor of Kansas City, who served from 1991 to 1999?

3. What U.S. senator from Missouri killed lawyer and politician Charles Lucas in a 1817 duel, only three years before he was first elected to congress?

4. St. Louisan Robert Hannegan put his stamp on what high-ranking federal government position under President Harry Truman?

5. Nicknamed "Boss Tom," what larger-than-life politician and his political machine ruled over Kansas City for more than twenty years starting in the 1920s?

6. Missouri Governor Harry S. Hadley took on which major oil company as Missouri's attorney general in 1906, when he prosecuted them for violations of anti-trust laws?

7. In 1884, Mark Twain's publishing company had a best seller when they published the memoirs of what one-time Missourian? (He was a famed military leader and a U.S. president.)

8. Kansas City political bosses Tom and James Pendergast were both in what business outside of politics?

9. What was the salary of the governor of Missouri in 2007?

    A. $95,000   B. $104,359   C. $129,922   D. $165,200

ANSWERS

BUSINESS & POLITICS

1. Kemper Arena

2. Emmanuel Cleaver II

3. Thomas Hart Benton

4. Postmaster General

5. Tom Pendergast

6. Standard Oil

7. Ulysses S. Grant

8. Saloon owners

9. C. $129,922

Business & Politics

1. What company, the second largest cinema chain in the United States, was founded in Kansas City in 1920?

2. What St. Louis–based hotel chain began with the opening of their first property in Sikeston in 1973?

3. What once nationwide chain of auto parts stores was founded in Kansas City in 1909?

4. What major baseball equipment manufacturer traces its roots back to a sporting goods store opened in downtown St. Louis in 1887?

5. What St. Louis–based grocery store chain began with the opening of its first store in 1939?

6. Manufacturing giant Leggett & Platt is headquartered in which southwest Missouri city?

7. Which major airline moved its headquarters from New York City to Kansas City in 1931?

8. What Kansas City–based company is the largest producer of baked goods in the United States?

9. Two St. Louis aircraft companies merged in 1967 to form what aerospace and defense contracting company?

10. Founded in Springfield in 1957, what auto parts chain now operates over 1,500 stores across the United States?

11. The headquarters of what Kansas City company has been located at the intersection of 18th and Grand since 1911?

ANSWERS

BUSINESS & POLITICS

1. AMC Theatres

2. Drury Hotels

3. Western Auto

4. Rawlings

5. Schnucks

6. Carthage

7. Trans World Airlines (TWA)

8. Interstate Bakeries Corporation

9. McDonnell Douglas

10. O'Reilly Auto Parts

11. *Kansas City Star*

BUSINESS & POLITICS

1. Located in Washington, Missouri, since 1869, the Missouri Meerschaum Company is the world's oldest and largest manufacturer of what tobacco-related product?

2. What major battery manufacturer has its headquarters in St. Louis?

3. Shelter Insurance, originally a subsidiary of the Missouri Farmer's Association (MFA), is headquartered in which Missouri city?

4. Carthage-based manufacturing giant Leggett & Platt began business by selling what product?

5. What St. Louis–based shoe company produces the Buster Brown, Naturalizer, and Dr. Scholl's lines of foot products and operates the Famous Footwear retail chain?

6. The Danforth family of St. Louis, which includes former Missouri Senator John "Jack" Danforth, made a fortune with what pet food company?

7. A well-known downtown hotel, a popular brand of beer, and a baseball stadium all bore the name of which industrious Kansas City family?

8. Who joined his father-in-law, Eberhard Anheuser, in the beer business in St. Louis in 1864?

9. What St. Louis native held various jobs around the country before returning to St. Louis in 1922 to open the first office of the stock brokerage company that still bears his name?

10. Missouri Governor Lloyd Stark's family business was one of the nation's largest producers of what type of fruit?

ANSWERS

BUSINESS & POLITICS

1. The corn cob smoking pipe

2. Energizer

3. Columbia

4. Steel bed springs

5. Brown Shoe Company

6. Ralston Purina

7. The Muehlebach family

8. Adolphus Busch

9. Edward D. Jones

10. Apples

BUSINESS & POLITICS

1. The co-founders of Wal-Mart, brothers Sam and Bud Walton, attended Hickman High School, which is located in what central Missouri city?

2. Originally called New Detroit, which eastern Missouri town was founded in the late nineteenth century to serve as a glass manufacturing center?

3. How many Missouri businesses made the 2008 "Fortune 500" list?

    A. 3   B. 5   C. 9   D. 15

4. What St. Louis businessman, who shares a name with his writer grandson, made a fortune when he invented the automated calculating machine in 1885?

5. Which Springfield hotel mogul worked as a teacher and in the construction business before developing his first hotel in 1958?

6. Real estate mogul J. C. Nichols developed what ritzy shopping district in Kansas City in 1923?

7. What leading tax preparation company was founded by two brothers in Kansas City in 1955?

8. Which Kansas City businessman made a fortune in pharmaceuticals before founding the Royals in 1968?

9. What large Missouri company traces its roots to the early nineteenth century when Nebraska-born brothers Joyce Clyde "J.C." and Rollie Hall began selling picture postcards in Kansas City?

ANSWERS

BUSINESS & POLITICS

1. Columbia

2. Crystal City

3. C. 9

4. William Seward Burroughs

5. John Q. Hammons

6. The Country Club Plaza

7. H&R Block

8. Ewing Kauffman

9. Hallmark

MISCELLANEOUS

Aviation and Missouri have had a long and storied relationship. From Air Force bases to jet fighter manufacturing to the man who invented the Lear Jet, the Show Me State has been at the forefront of air travel. And of course, there is the Spirit of St. Louis. The first transcontinental airplane trip was conceived and planned right here in the Show Me State. But there is a story behind that first flight that few people are aware of.

In the early 1900s, there was a St. Louis–based company known as Lambert Pharmaceuticals. Their best-known product was a bad breath antiseptic known as Listerine. Listerine became a household product in the 1920s thanks to an ad campaign that alerted Americans to the perils of bad breath. It was just one of several products marketed by Lambert at that time, but it was the one item that made the family fabulously wealthy.

The large amount of money the family made from Listerine allowed Jordan Lambert's son, Albert Bond Lambert, to grow up in the lap of luxury. He grew accustomed to the finer things in life, including the newest pastime sweeping America: aviation. He was active in clubs for hot air ballooning and flying airplanes, where he and his well-to-do friends would pursue their passion in the skies. They even formed the St. Louis Aero Club, which built the city's first airfield. Lambert eventually purchased a piece of property twenty miles northwest of the St. Louis city limits. That piece of land in the "country" eventually became Lambert Field.

At Lambert Field, he met and befriended another young pilot named Charles Lindbergh. Lambert believed in this young man's ability as well as his dream to fly across the Atlantic. So

Lambert began raising money to make the Spirit of St. Louis a reality. He convinced his wealthy friends in St. Louis to back the venture. The dream came true in 1927 as Lindbergh flew the Spirit of St. Louis across the Atlantic from New York to Paris.

The sky was now literally limit for the future of aviation. The excitement generated by this amazing feat (which most everyone thought would fail), generated an incredible interest in commercial aviation around the world. The fact that the historic *Spirit of St. Louis* flight originated from Missouri also helped boost the aviation industry across the state. In the end, although it may be hard to believe, Missouri became ground zero for aviation in the early years of air travel, thanks in large part to bad breath!

MISCELLANEOUS

MIXED BAG

1. How many covered bridges are still standing in Missouri?

   A. 4   B. 9   C. 15   D. 22

2. What is the nickname of the seven-foot-tall sasquatch that numerous Missourians have claimed to have seen roaming the Missouri wilderness since the 1970s?

3. Twelve Harley Davidsons, three Indian, and two Henderson motorcycles were among the original fleet of what Missouri law enforcement agency?

4. According to the 2000 Census, Missouri's per capita income of $19,936 ranks where among the nation's fifty states in terms of highest income?

   A. 15th   B. 19th   C. 25th   D. 30th

5. What stubborn four-legged animal became the official animal of Missouri in 1995?

6. The Black Archives of Mid-America, a resource and showcase of African-American history in the Midwest, is located in which Missouri city?

7. The Missouri Lottery began operations in what year?

   A. 1977   B. 1980   C. 1985   D. 1990

ANSWERS

MIXED BAG

1. A. 4

2. Momo the Monster

3. The Missouri State Highway Patrol

4. D. 30th

5. The Missouri Mule

6. Kansas City

7. C. 1985

MISCELLANEOUS

TRANSPORTATION

1. Kansas City International Airport is identified by what three-letter acronym on maps and navigational charts?

2. Theodore Roosevelt became the first U.S. president to fly when he took a short airplane ride during a Wright brothers exhibition in which Missouri city in 1910?

3. Interstate 670 in Kansas City is named for what prominent K.C. businessman who headed the Kansas City Stockyards for over twenty-five years?

4. In what year did MetroLink, St. Louis's light-rail transportation system, begin operations?

5. The first railroad tracks in Kansas City were laid by which railroad in 1865?

6. What famous St. Louis bridge was the longest arch bridge in the world when it was completed in 1874?

7. Before it became the international airport in St. Louis, Kinloch Field was used as a launching site for what type of aircraft?

8. What form of transportation did many Kansas Citians of the late nineteenth and early twentieth centuries use to get from downtown Kansas City to the West Bottoms neighborhood?

9. What road, which connects St. Louis and St. Charles, was first paved with stones in 1865?

ANSWERS

TRANSPORTATION

1. MCI

2. St. Louis

3. Jay Dillingham

4. 1993

5. Missouri Pacific

6. Eads Bridge

7. Hot air balloons

8. Cable cars

9. St. Charles Rock Road

MISCELLANEOUS

NEWSPAPERS

Match each of the cities listed below with the major newspaper published there.

1. St. Joseph   A. *Democrat*

2. Springfield   B. *Globe*

3. Independence   C. *Daily Tribune*

4. Joplin   D. *Post-Dispatch*

5. Jefferson City   E. *News-Press*

6. Sedalia   F. *Examiner*

7. Columbia   G. *Star*

8. St. Louis   H. *News-Leader*

9. Lee's Summit   I. *Journal*

10. Kansas City   J. *News Tribune*

ANSWERS

NEWSPAPERS

1. E. *St. Joseph News-Press*

2. H. *Springfield News-Leader*

3. F. *Independence Examiner*

4. B. *Joplin Globe*

5. J. *Jefferson City News Tribune*

6. A. *Sedalia Democrat*

7. C. *Columbia Daily Tribune*

8. D. *St. Louis Post-Dispatch*

9. I. *Lee's Summit Journal*

10. G. *Kansas City Star*

MISCELLANEOUS

MIXED BAG

1. What animated character said: "I'll be deep in the cold, cold ground before I recognize Missouri," when asked to explain why he owned an American flag with only 49 stars on it?

2. The world's largest freshwater diving resort is located in an abandoned lead mine in what eastern Missouri town?

3. Immortalized with both a book and a memorial garden, Jim the Wonder Dog lived in which central Missouri town?

4. What Kansas City amusement park was built by Kansas City Chiefs owner Lamar Hunt in 1973?

5. Which relatively short, flower-producing tree became Missouri's official tree in 1955?

6. Senator Willard D. Vandiver is often credited with popularizing what nickname for the state of Missouri during an 1899 speech?

7. Which state correctional facility in southeastern Missouri housed Missouri's death row from 1989 until 2005?

8. What high-flying event has been held at Pershing State Park near Brookfield every Labor Day since 1977?

9. What major Missouri event was first held in September of 1901 in Sedalia?

ANSWERS

MIXED BAG

1. Abe Simpson (Grandpa on *The Simpsons*)

2. Bonne Terre

3. Marshall

4. Worlds of Fun

5. The Flowering Dogwood

6. The Show Me State

7. The Potosi Correctional Center

8. The Great Pershing Balloon Derby

9. The Missouri State Fair

MISCELLANEOUS

MIXED BAG

1. What valuable decorative stone has been mined in and around Carthage since the late 1800s?

2. How many city parks are located in St. Louis City?

     A. 52   B. 80   C. 105   D. 133

3. In 1904, Elwood, a thoroughbred racehorse from Maryville, became the only Missouri-based horse to win what prestigious sporting event?

4. The United States Junior Chamber (Jaycees) club was founded in 1920 in which Missouri city?

5. Alexander Majors and George Caleb Bingham are both buried in what large Kansas City cemetery?

6. The National World War I Museum is located on the grounds of what Kansas City landmark? (The landmark itself is the national World War I memorial.)

7. What national student organization was founded at the Baltimore Hotel in downtown Kansas City in 1928?

8. From 1891 to 1911, Missourian Walter Wyman served in what highest-ranking public health position within the federal government?

9. The United States Medical Center for Federal Prisoners is located in which Missouri city?

ANSWERS

MIXED BAG

1. Marble

2. C. 105

3. The Kentucky Derby

4. St. Louis

5. Union Cemetery

6. The Liberty Memorial

7. FFA (Future Farmers of America)

8. Surgeon General

9. Springfield

MISCELLANEOUS

ANIMALS

1. What is the largest animal currently roaming the wilds of Missouri?

2. Clarksville, located on the Mississippi River in northeastern Missouri, is a popular place to see what kind of majestic bird? (They flock to the area during the winter.)

3. How many species of lizards live in Missouri?

      A. 2   B. 7   C. 10   D. 13

4. How many species of venomous snakes live in Missouri?

      A. 2   B. 5   C. 7   D. 12

5. What urban park is home to the St. Louis Zoo?

6. The Kansas City Zoo is located in what park?

7. Built with the help of the Works Progress Administration in the 1930s, the Dickerson Park Zoo is located in which Missouri city?

8. Bennet Spring State Park, Roaring River State Park, Montauk State Park, and Meramec Spring Park are all popular areas for anglers hoping to catch what game fish?

9. What abundant and tasty fish became the official fish of the state of Missouri in 1997?

ANSWERS

ANIMALS

1. The Black Bear

2. The Bald Eagle

3. D. 13

4. B. 5

5. Forest Park

6. Swope Park

7. Springfield

8. Trout

9. The Channel Catfish

MISCELLANEOUS

MUSEUMS

1. Which St. Joseph hotel served as the headquarters of the Pony Express? (It is now a museum dedicated to the Pony Express and the history of St. Joseph.)

2. What St. Louis attraction began when philanthropist Henry Shaw opened his elaborate gardens to the public in 1859?

3. The campus of State Fair Community College in Sedalia is home to what renowned contemporary art museum?

4. What Kansas City art museum sits on the site of the former home of *Kansas City Star* founder William Rockhill Nelson?

5. In what city is the Missouri Sports Hall of Fame located?

6. What metropolitan area is home to the Museum of Transportation?

7. What Independence museum opened on July 6, 1957?

8. The Glore Psychiatric Museum, which illustrates the history of treating mental illness, is located on the campus of a former psychiatric hospital in what northwest Missouri city?

9. The Missouri History Museum is located in what St. Louis park?

10. What children's museum is located in the former International Shoe building in downtown St. Louis?

ANSWERS

MUSEUMS

1. Patee House

2. The Missouri Botanical Garden

3. The Daum Museum of Contemporary Art

4. The Nelson-Atkins Museum of Art

5. Springfield

6. St. Louis

7. The Harry S. Truman Library and Museum

8. St. Joseph

9. Forest Park

10. The City Museum

MISCELLANEOUS

NEWSPAPERS

1. What daily newspaper is written, photographed, and designed by journalism students at the University of Missouri?

2. *The Missouri Gazette*, first published by Joseph Charless in St. Louis in 1808, holds what distinction among Missouri's newspapers?

3. *The Missouri Gazette* was published in English and what other language?

4. Which religious group published *The Morning and Evening Star* in Independence in the 1830s?

5. One of the first Polish newspapers in the United States, *The Polish Eagle*, was established in 1870 in what east-central Missouri river town?

6. What is the name of the official student newspaper at the University of Missouri?

7. What two Missouri newspapers were purchased and consolidated by Joseph Pulitzer in 1879?

8. What Kansas City morning newspaper was purchased by *Kansas City Star* publisher William Rockhill Nelson in 1904?

9. What St. Louis newspaper, published from 1852 until 1986, was the *St. Louis Post-Dispatch*'s chief competitor?

10. What St. Louis–born journalist and poet was once the editor of *The Kansas City Times*?

11. In what year was *The Kansas City Star* first published?
    A. 1815   B. 1837   C. 1868   D. 1880

ANSWERS

NEWSPAPERS

1. *The Columbia Missourian*

2. It was the first published in Missouri

3. French

4. Latter Day Saints (Mormons)

5. Washington

6. *The Maneater*

7. *The St. Louis Post* and *The St. Louis Dispatch*

8. *The Kansas City Times*

9. *The St. Louis Globe-Democrat*

10. Eugene Field

11. D. 1880

MISCELLANEOUS

MIXED BAG

1. Which two Missouri towns each claim to hold the world's shortest St. Patrick's Day parade?

2. On August 10, 1821, Missouri became the ___th state admitted to the union?

   A. 16   B. 22   C. 24   D. 32

3. A statue of what famous comic strip character, created by Mizzou alum Mort Walker, sits on a bench on the University of Missouri campus near the former location of a bar and hangout known as "The Shack"?

4. What now-defunct amusement park, which was located on Prospect Avenue in Kansas City, was a popular regional attraction that operated from 1923 until 1977?

5. What large rodeo and animal show is held annually at Kemper and Hale Arenas in Kansas City?

6. The Soulard neighborhood in St. Louis is known for hosting parades and parties celebrating what February holiday?

7. Which urban St. Louis park is the oldest west of the Mississippi?

8. What colorful bird became the official state bird of Missouri in 1927?

ANSWERS

MIXED BAG

1. Maryville and Blue Springs

2. B. 24

3. Beetle Bailey

4. Fairyland Park

5. The American Royal

6. Mardi Gras

7. Lafayette Park

8. The Bluebird

MISCELLANEOUS

EDUCATION

1. Before its name change in 2005, Missouri State University in Springfield was known by what name?

2. What was the University of Central Missouri known as prior to its 2006 name change?

3. Missouri Governor Joseph Teasdale, pitcher David Cone, and film director Robert Altman all attended what Catholic high school in Kansas City?

4. What college, established in a small Ozarks town near Jefferson City in 1961, educates students in over twenty-five two-year technical programs?

5. What four-year college in Columbia was established in 1833 as the Columbia Female Academy?

6. What was Joplin Junior College renamed in 1968 when it became a four-year college?

7. What southwest Missouri university was established in 1873 as Springfield College?

8. What college was known as Fulton College when it was founded in 1849?

9. What St. Louis–area college was formerly known as Loretto College?

10. What university was established in 1915 as St. Joseph Junior College?

11. What Kansas City Jesuit university was founded in 1910?

ANSWERS

EDUCATION

1. Southwest Missouri State University

2. Central Missouri State University

3. Rockhurst

4. Linn State Technical College

5. Stephens College

6. Missouri Southern State University

7. Drury University

8. Westminster College

9. Webster University

10. Missouri Western State University

11. Rockhurst University

MISCELLANEOUS

TRANSPORTATION

1. Which aviation pioneer, whose surname is still a part of St. Louis aviation, purchased an airplane from the Wright Brothers and was the first St. Louisan to acquire a pilot's license?

2. What is the original name of Kansas City International Airport?

3. What road, which connected St. Louis and New Madrid, became the first official road in Missouri when it was platted by Spanish officials in 1789?

4. Both of the Amtrak passenger trains that make daily round trips between St. Louis and Kansas City are named for what Missouri animal?

5. One of the longest of what type of early hard-surfaced roads was built in 1851 between Ste. Genevieve and Iron Mountain?

6. In 1852, the first passenger train service in Missouri carried riders the five miles from Cheltenham to what city?

7. Kansas City's first Union Station was located in which industrial neighborhood?

8. What Missouri law enforcement agency is responsible for regulating Missouri's waterways and maintaining the safety of those who use them?

9. In operation since 1853, the ferry in what northeastern Missouri town is the longest continually running ferry across the Mississippi River?

ANSWERS

TRANSPORTATION

1. Albert Lambert

2. Mid-Continent International Airport

3. El Camino Real (The King's Highway)

4. The Mule (The St. Louis Mule and the Kansas City Mule)

5. Plank Road

6. St. Louis

7. The West Bottoms

8. The Missouri State Water Patrol

9. Canton

MISCELLANEOUS

MIXED BAG

1. Highlandville, Missouri, is home to which of the following?

    A. The world's largest green pepper

    B. The world's shortest road

    C. The world's largest musket

    D. The world's smallest cathedral

2. What Ozark Mountain area, near Alton, is named for the ethnicity of a group of families who settled there in the 1850s?

3. The Katy Trail is built on the trackbed of what now-defunct railroad?

4. The U.S. Air Force's fleet of B-2 Stealth Bombers are stationed at what central Missouri military base?

5. What famous talking car, a 1931 Model A Ford Roadster, first taught Missourians about auto safety at the Missouri State Fair in Sedalia in 1969?

6. The original headstone from the grave of what great American patriot and U.S. president is now located on the quad at the University of Missouri?

7. Launched by Margaret Truman in 1944, what famous battleship served the U.S. Navy for seventeen years?

8. Artist Thomas Hart Benton was an art instructor at what Missouri educational institution?

ANSWERS

MIXED BAG

1. D. The world's smallest cathedral

2. The Irish Wilderness

3. The Missouri-Kansas-Texas (MKT) Railroad

4. Whiteman Air Force Base

5. Otto the Talking Car

6. Thomas Jefferson

7. The USS *Missouri*

8. The Kansas City Art Institute

MISCELLANEOUS

WEATHER

1. What is the coldest temperature ever recorded in Missouri?

    A. -12° F   B. -22° F   C. -40° F   D. -44° F

2. What is the warmest temperature ever recorded in Missouri?

    A. 112° F   B. 118° F   C. 122° F   D. 125° F

3. Approximately how many inches of precipitation fell on Portageville in 1957? (It was the most ever recorded in one year in Missouri.)

    A. 70   B. 84   C. 89   D. 92

4. The world record for rainfall was set in Holt, Missouri, in 1947. How many inches of rain fell there in forty-two minutes?

    A. 7   B. 9   C. 12   D. 16

5. According to the National Oceanic and Atmospheric Administration (NOAA), what is the average number of tornadoes that touched down annually in Missouri from 1953 to 2004?

    A. 18   B. 22   C. 30   D. 44

6. The largest hailstone ever recorded in Missouri fell near Meadville in May of 2004. What was the diamater (in inches) of the hailstone?

    A. 2   B. 6   C. 9   D. 12

ANSWERS

WEATHER

1. C. -40° F

2. B. 118° F

3. D. 92 inches

4. C. 12 inches

5. C. 30

6. B. 6

MISCELLANEOUS

EDUCATION

1. Established in 1880, what military academy in central Missouri is the oldest military academy west of the Mississippi River?

2. What was the official name of the university in Kirksville before it became Truman State University in 1996?

3. The first journalism school in the world opened where in 1908?

4. Which military academy opened its doors in 1889 after local citizens donated land and money for its construction?

5. Poet T. S. Eliot's grandfather, William Greenleaf Eliot, was one of the co-founders of which St. Louis university?

6. A college in Liberty was named for which Columbia resident, who donated $10,000 for the establishment of the school?

7. How many students were in the University of Missouri's first graduating class in 1843?

> A. 1   B. 2   C. 6   D. 15

8. In 1873, Susan Blow opened the first public kindergarten in the U.S. in which Missouri city?

9. What Springfield high school is named for an Indian tribe who once occupied the prairie where the school now sits?

ANSWERS

EDUCATION

1. Wentworth Military Academy

2. Northeast Missouri State University

3. The University of Missouri

4. Missouri Military Academy (Mexico)

5. Washington University

6. William Jewell

7. B. 2

8. St. Louis

9. Kickapoo High School

MISCELLANEOUS

MIXED BAG

1. A half-scale replica of what famous prehistoric monument is located on the campus of the Missouri University of Science and Technology in Rolla?

2. According to the U.S. Census Bureau what was the estimated population of Missouri in 2008?

   A. 2,554,208   B. 3,899,454   C. 5,911,605   D. 7,303,250

3. The University of Missouri was modeled, in part, after what university in the eastern United States?

4. "Maxie," the world's largest goose, can be found in a park in what small town near central Missouri's Swan Lake National Wildlife Refuge?

5. Which route, the longest state highway in Missouri, stretches from Iowa to Arkansas and passes through the towns of Milan, Marceline, Boonville, Versailles, Lebanon, and Ava?

6. What Missouri law enforcement agency began operations in 1931 with a total of fifty-five officers?

7. Which covered bridge, located at a historic site near Pershing Park, is the longest of the covered bridges remaining in Missouri?

8. What famous Oklahoma-born cowboy, comedian, writer, and actor attended Kemper Military Academy in Boonville in the 1890s?

9. A deep chasm at Grand Gulf State Park near Thayer was formed by the collapse of what type of geological feature?

ANSWERS

MIXED BAG

1. Stonehenge

2. C. 5,911,605

3. The University of Virginia

4. Sumner

5. Missouri Route 5

6. The Missouri State Highway Patrol

7. Locust Creek Covered Bridge

8. Will Rogers

9. A cave

MISCELLANEOUS

TRANSPORTATION

1. In 1903, the first speed limit in Missouri was set at how many miles per hour?

    A. 5   B. 9   C. 12   D. 15

2. Kansas City's downtown airport is named for which Kansas City mayor who held the office from 1971 until 1979?

3. The world's first gas station was established in 1905 in which Missouri city?

4. Which Kansas City transportation landmark was built in low-lying land just south of downtown in 1914?

5. How many miles of highway are there in Missouri?

    A. 10,255   B. 22,438   C. 32,340   D. 47,887

6. What romanticized American highway began its Missouri portion in St. Louis and ran southwest, exiting the state west of Joplin?

7. Which Missouri airport became the first municipally owned airport in the United States in 1928?

ANSWERS

TRANSPORTATION

1. B. 9

2. Charles Wheeler

3. St. Louis

4. Union Station

5. C. 32,340

6. Route 66

7. Lambert International Airport

MISCELLANEOUS

FOOD AND DRINK

1. Michelob beer was first introduced by Anheuser-Busch in what year?

>   A. 1896   B. 1922   C. 1955   D. 1964

2. What Kansas City brewery was founded by John McDonald in 1989?

3. What popular Anheuser-Busch product was first introduced in 1955?

4. What brand of salad dressing was introduced by a former petroleum engineer in his Carthage restaurant in the 1940s?

5. What popular Italian appetizer is said to have been invented in "the Hill" neighborhood in St. Louis?

6. In what year was Budweiser beer first available in cans?

>   A. 1912   B. 1922   C. 1936   D. 1948

7. What variety of green apple was popularized by the Stark Brothers Nursery of Louisiana, Missouri, in the early twentieth century?

8. What cherry-chocolate treat has been produced by Chase Candy Company of St. Joseph since 1918?

ANSWERS

FOOD AND DRINK

1. A. 1896

2. Boulevard Brewing Company

3. Busch Beer

4. Ott's Famous Salad Dressing

5. Toasted ravioli

6. C. 1936

7. Golden Delicious

8. Cherry Mash

MISCELLANEOUS

FOOD AND DRINK

1. Columbia residents and Mizzou students have been shooting pool, drinking beer, and eating burgers served on wax paper in what popular tavern and pool hall in downtown Columbia since 1884?

2. What popular Chinese restaurant staple was created and popularized in the 1950s by David Leong of Springfield?

3. What was the name of the popular non-alcoholic beer brewed by Anheuser-Busch during the Prohibition era?

4. What iconic West Bottoms steakhouse was opened by Kansas City Stockyards President Jay Dillingham in 1955?

5. In 1928, the first "sliced bread" was offered for sale in which northwestern Missouri town?

6. What spirits manufacturer traces its roots back to 1856 when Ben Holladay began making whiskey at his distillery located just outside of Weston?

7. Oak wood from the forests near Perryville is used by a French company to manufacture what product related to the alcoholic beverage industry?

8. What well-known producer of cured hams, bacon, sausage, and other specialty meats began operations on a farm outside of California, Missouri, in 1952?

9. In what year was Budweiser beer first introduced?

      A. 1860   B. 1876   C. 1904   D. 1916

ANSWERS

FOOD AND DRINK

1. Booches

2. Cashew Chicken

3. Bevo

4. The Golden Ox

5. Chillicothe

6. McCormick Distilling Company

7. Wine barrels

8. Stone Hill Winery

9. B. 1876

MISCELLANEOUS

FOOD AND DRINK

1. What popular lemon-lime soft drink was developed in St. Louis by Charles Leiper Grigg in 1929?

2. What frozen custard shop has been serving up their famous treat on Chippewa Street in St. Louis every summer since 1941?

3. The Griesedieck family starting making what popular root beer brand in St. Louis during Prohibition in 1919?

4. The Wheel Inn, formerly located at the intersection of Highways 65 and 50 in Sedalia, was well known for serving what odd sandwich?

5. What restaurant, one of the two most famous barbeque joints in Kansas City, first opened its doors in 1946 at the intersection of 19th and Vine?

6. The original Lambert's Cafe, home of "throwed rolls," is located in what southeastern Missouri town?

7. What regional pizzeria chain, famous for their thin-crust, square-cut, St. Louis–style pizzas, was founded with a single location at Thurman and Shaw in St. Louis in 1964?

8. What Kansas City chain of burger restaurants, known for their steak burgers, opened their first Kansas City–area restaurant near the County Club Plaza in 1940?

9. Backer's potato chips are manufactured in what central Missouri town?

ANSWERS

FOOD AND DRINK

1. 7-UP

2. Ted Drewes

3. IBC Root Beer

4. The Goober Burger (A hamburger topped with peanut butter)

5. Gates Barbeque

6. Sikeston

7. Imo's

8. Winstead's

9. Fulton

Miscellaneous

At the Fair?

Six of the items listed below are said to have been introduced or popularized at the 1904 World's Fair in St. Louis, and six were not. All you have to do is decide "at the Fair" or "not at the Fair."

1. The ice cream cone

2. Cappuccino

3. Root Beer

4. Dr. Pepper

5. The hot dog

6. Funnel cakes

7. Corn dogs

8. Cotton Candy

9. Doughnuts

10. Iced tea

11. The hamburger

12. Tater tots

ANSWERS

AT THE FAIR?

1. At the fair

2. Not at the fair

3. Not at the fair

4. At the fair

5. At the fair

6. Not at the fair

7. Not at the fair

8. At the fair

9. Not at the fair

10. At the fair

11. At the fair

12. Not at the fair

MISCELLANEOUS

FOOD AND DRINK

1. What Liberty-based snack company was founded by Guy Caldwell and family in 1938?

2. What are the two best-selling beers in the world?

3. What sandwich, made popular in St. Louis–area Chinese restaurants, is usually made up of egg foo young, lettuce, tomato, pickle and mayonnaise on two slices of white bread?

4. What popular Italian-style salad dressing was first made and popularized in the 1940s and 1950s at Phillip Sollomi's Kansas City restaurant? (The restaurant and the dressing share the same name.)

5. The first location of which small Kansas City steakhouse chain opened in 1957?

6. Falstaff Beer was first brewed at which St. Louis brewery?

7. Which famous barbeque joint, located at 18th and Brooklyn in Kansas City, was founded in the early 1920s by the brother of the restaurant's namesake?

8. What pancake mix brand was first introduced in St. Joseph in 1889?

9. What type of cheese is typically used on a St. Louis–style pizza?

10. What writer for The New Yorker once wrote that "... the single best restaurant in the world is Arthur Bryant's Barbeque at 18th & Brooklyn in Kansas City"?

ANSWERS

FOOD AND DRINK

1. Guy's Snacks

2. Budweiser and Bud Light

3. The St. Paul Sandwich

4. Wish Bone

5. Hereford House

6. The Lemp Brewing Company

7. Arthur Bryant's

8. Aunt Jemima

9. Provel

10. Calvin Trillin